curriculum connections

Native North Americans

Peoples of the Southwest, West, and North

BROWN BEAR BOOKS

Published by Brown Bear Books Limited

An imprint of:
The Brown Reference Group Ltd
68 Topstone Road
Redding
Connecticut 06896
USA
www.brownreference.com

© 2009 The Brown Reference Group Ltd

ISBN: 978-1-933834-78-8

Editorial Director: Lindsey Lowe
Senior Managing Editor: Tim Cooke
Managing Editor: Laura Durman
Editor: Rebecca Hunter
Designer: Barry Dwyer

Library of Congress Cataloging-in-Publication Data available upon request

Picture Credits

Cover Image
Shutterstock/July Flower

vera bogaerts/Shutterstock: p.95; George Burba/Shutterstock: p.42; Karoline Cullen/Shutterstock: p.33; Gordon Galbraith/Shutterstock: p.98; Jupiter Images: pp.7, 54, 79; John Kropewnicki/Shutterstock: p.9; Library of Congress: pp. 14 (Edward S. Curtis Collection), 36 (Detroit Photographic Co.), 39 (Frank E. Kleinschmidt), 47 (Edward S. Curtis Collection), 68 (William M. Pennington and Wesley R. Rowland), 73, 76 (Edward S. Curtis Collection), 105 (Edward S. Curtis Collection); Geir Olav Lyngfjell/Shutterstock: p.10; Tomasz Otap/Shutterstock: p.23; Michael Rahel/Shutterstock: p.51; Weldon Schloneger/Shutterstock: p.90; Andrew Tichovolsky/Shutterstock: p.53

Artwork © The Brown Reference Group Ltd

The Brown Reference Group Ltd has made every effort to trace copyright holders of the pictures used in this book. Anyone having claims to ownership not identified above is invited to contact The Brown Reference Group Ltd.

Printed in the United States of America

Contents

Introduction

Native North Americans forms part of the Curriculum Connections project. The six volumes of the set cover all aspects of the history and culture of native peoples in what are now the United States and Canada. Each volume covers a particular aspect of Native American life: Peoples of the East, Southeast, and Plains; Peoples of the Southwest, West, and North; Arts, Society, and Religion; History; Personalities and Places; and Warfare, Economy, and Technology.

About this set

Each volume in *Native North Americans* features a series of articles arranged in A–Z order. The articles are all listed in the contents pages of each book, and can also be located through the indexes.

Each illustrated article provides a concise but accurate summary of its subject, accompanied where relevant by informative maps. Articles about major tribes are each accompanied by a fact file that provides a summary of essential information.

Within each article, two key aids to learning are located in sidebars in the margins of each page:

Curriculum Context sidebars indicate that a subject has particular relevance to state and national American history guidelines and curricula. They highlight essential information or suggest useful ways for students to include a subject in their studies.

Glossary sidebars define key words within the text.

At the end of the book, a summary Glossary lists the key terms defined in the volume. There is also a list of further print and Web-based resources and a full volume index.

About this volume

This book studies the various native peoples who inhabited the western and northern parts of North America: the Arctic circle and Alaska, the Pacific Northwest, the Plateau and the Columbia Basin, the Southwest, California, and Mexico. It covers a wide range of cultures, from the urban empires of the Aztec to the Inuit who hunted seal and polar bear on the frozen sea of the Arctic circle. In the deserts of the Southwest native peoples learned how to exploit scarce natural resources and use irrigation to live in an environment that still remains daunting today.

The West Coast had different lifestyles from the East, particularly after the arrival of Europeans. Here, the early European influence was Spanish, as expressed by the missions of California and particularly by the introduction of the horse—introduced to the Americas by Spaniards via Mexico—to the peoples of the Southwest and the Plains. Other influences were the Russians in Alaska and the French in British Columbia.

Some native peoples resisted European encroachment. The Pueblo of the desert Southwest mounted one of the few successful revolts against the newcomers, while conflict between other peoples and U.S. settlers led to intense conflict with the U.S. Army throughout most of the 19th century. By 1900, however, the native peoples had been subdued. Many were confined to reservations of marginal land where farming was difficult. However, later in the 20th century some tribes were able to take advantage of tribal self-government in order to exploit mineral resources and run successful casinos for gambling.

Acoma

Acoma is the name of both a people and their village. The Acoma village lies within a reservation in west-central New Mexico. It sits on a high plateau and claims to be the oldest continuously inhabited site in North America.

The Acoma dwellings are pueblo, which are adjoining structures made of stone and adobe (clay and straw), and are traditional native buildings in the region. The village—a National Historic Landmark—has been inhabited since 1075 CE. Today, most Acoma people live in farming villages near the ancient site, but several families still live within the village itself.

The villagers speak Keresan. The name *Acoma* is a Spanish word based on the Keresan word *Akome*, which means "People of the White Rock."

Farmers and Craftspeople

The Acoma used to be farmers. They still keep some animals and grow a few crops, and some families still make their delicate, decorated pottery, which is among the finest of Native American crafts.

Well into the 16th century, there were several tribes who lived peacefully in small villages throughout the region. They grew corn and squash, tended their animals, and observed unique religious rituals.

In Acoma, everything was owned by the women, and a person's descent was traced through the mother's side of the family. The men's role was to hunt and to attend to the community's religious life.

Arrival of the Spanish

In 1540, a Spanish expedition led by Francisco Vasquez de Coronado made the first European contact with the Acoma. However, it was an event in 1598 that changed

National Historic Landmark

A structure, site, or district recognized by the U.S government for its historical significance.

Curriculum Context

It may be revealing to compare gender roles in different Native American societies.

the Acoma's way of life forever. Juan de Zaldivar was leading 30 men across the desert when they stopped at Acoma and insisted that the village provide them with food for their journey. The Acoma agreed to grind corn for the Spanish, who waited outside the village on the desert-valley floor.

After three days, Zaldivar grew impatient, and the Spanish climbed the giant rock and stormed Acoma. The villagers fought back and killed all but four of the Spanish. The next month, Zaldivar's brother Vincente arrived with 70 Spaniards seeking revenge. They hoisted a cannon up the rock face and killed 1,500 Acoma (half of the population).

For many years, native peoples of the Southwest suffered under Spanish rule. However, in 1680, the Acoma joined the Pueblo Rebellion, destroying the Spanish army post at Santa Fe and keeping the Spanish out of the region for 12 years.

Pueblo Rebellion
A planned uprising of Pueblo peoples against Spanish colonization in August 1680. Many Spanish settlers and Franciscan priests were killed, and the Spanish fled from the city of Santa Fe.

Modern Acoma
Today, the Acoma perform a number of festivals and celebrations that visitors can attend. Many take place during the summer months. In September, the Acoma have their most popular festival, the feast of San Estevan, which celebrates their patron saint.

Acoma village was built on a steep-sided sandstone plateau that rises 360 feet (110 m) from the desert-valley floor. The Acoma call the village Ako, but it is popularly known as Sky City.

Anasazi

The Anasazi (meaning the "ancient ones") were the ancestors of the majority of the Pueblo who still live in the Rio Grande Valley of New Mexico. The Anasazi produced large amounts of basketry and fiber weavings and are therefore sometimes known today as the Basketmaker Culture, particularly in their early period.

Pottery, which centuries later was to become the most important Pueblo craftwork, was first produced by the Anasazi in about 500 CE. These early pieces were greatly influenced by the ceramic traditions of two of their neighbors to the south, the Mogollon and the Hohokam peoples.

Ancient Dwellings

By about 700 CE, the Anasazi had a new and distinctive black-on-white pottery style. This period also saw a change in their type of housing. Before this period, the Anasazi lived mostly in shallow pits covered with a pole-and-brush roof. But during this time, they began to move above ground into apartments built from adobe (dried mud bricks) or stone.

However, the circular pit-house remained important. Dug deeper than before, it became a wholly underground circular chamber with a rooftop entrance through what was previously the smokehole of the house. These chambers are known as kivas, and they became ceremonial meeting places maintained by male members of the clans or tribes.

Clan
A social unit consisting of a number of households or families with a common ancestor.

Cliff Houses

Anasazi culture reached its peak about 1100. Before this date, most villages consisted of compact clusters of houses built on mesa, or plateau, tops. However, by about 1150, nearly all the buildings in the Anasazi area, such as those at Mesa Verde in New Mexico, were being built inside recesses in cliffs. This gave the Anasazi greater protection and shelter. One of the largest surviving examples of a cliff dwelling is Cliff Palace in Mesa Verde. It contains more than 200 rooms and 23 kivas built within a natural rock shelter.

Access to Cliff Palace was difficult and could be achieved only by a hard climb down steep, rough paths and ladders from the mesa top. Yet the high number of kivas suggests that Cliff Palace was not only a working settlement but that it also functioned as a ceremonial center for outlying communities.

This arrangement was probably also the case for the majority of the larger Anasazi settlements, suggesting it was a society based on a widespread network of trade, family, and social relationships.

Harsh Climate

Agriculture was central to the Anasazi, but water was scarce in the dry Southwest. To harness what little water there was, the Anasazi constructed complex storage systems, including artificial ponds and lakes and deep cisterns.

Curriculum Context

It may be interesting to consider the practicalities of day-to-day life in a dwelling such as the Cliff Palace.

Cliff Palace in Mesa Verde National Park, Colorado, is the largest cliff dwelling in North America. Archaeologists believe that it contained two communities, linked by a kiva in the middle, which was plastered in two different colors on opposing sides.

Water storage was vital to the Anasazi, and long droughts had a major impact on their history. A 23-year-long drought between 1276 and 1299 is generally believed to be the reason for the abandonment of the cliff dwellings in 1300.

Spanish Impact

The abandonment of the cliff dwellings was followed some 100 or 200 years later by the arrival of nomadic hunters and raiders in the Southwest, the ancestors of the modern Apache and Navajo. They in turn were followed by the Spanish, who traveled from Mexico in search of gold. Although the Spanish did not discover the riches they sought, their presence and religious intolerance undermined the cultural traditions and patterns of the Native Americans.

Despite the harsh environment of the Southwest and the impact of European settlers on the region, various Native American cultures survived. As testament to the ancient tribe's accomplishments, many of the agricultural methods and beliefs of the Anasazi continue to be practiced by the Pueblo.

Nomadic

Having no permanent home and moving from one place to another according to the seasons in search of hunting grounds, water, and grazing land.

Newspaper Rock State Historic Monument in Utah features Anasazi petroglyphs among its carvings, which were created over many hundreds of years. The pictures include depictions of people riding horses.

Apache

The name *Apache* refers to a group of six closely related tribes: Chiricahua, Kiowa–Apache, Lipan, Western Apache, Jicarilla, and Mescalero. We know that they were all descended from a group of people who spoke the Athapascan language.

Having migrated from the Subarctic sometime after 825 CE, the Apache were among the last groups to arrive in the Southwest—shortly before the first Spanish conquistadors in the 16th century.

The word *Apache* comes from a Zuni word meaning "enemy"—the Zuni were their neighbors—but they referred to themselves as *Dine* (the people). At first, the Apache were hostile toward peoples already living in the Southwest and soon carved out their own territory.

Colonizing the Southwest

Later, the Kiowa–Apache settled on the fringes of the Great Plains, where they merged with the Kiowa and became full-time buffalo hunters. The Lipan settled on the southern Plains, displacing the Comanche. The remaining tribes settled in the Southwest's mountains, dividing roughly into western and eastern groups. The Western Apache and Chiricahua moved into the old Anasazi and Mogollon homelands, where they hunted deer and antelope. The Apache tribes that settled in the east—the Jicarilla and Mescalero—hunted buffalo. The Eastern Apache also farmed a small amount of corn, beans, and squash.

Enter the Spanish

The first white intruders were the Spanish in the late 1500s. As they moved northward, they disrupted Apache trade with neighboring tribes. When New Mexico became a Spanish colony in 1598, hostilities between the Spaniards and Apache increased. The Spanish brought horses, which quickly became part of

Conquistador

The Spanish word for "conqueror," used to describe the early Spanish soldiers, explorers, and adventurers involved in the conquest of the Americas.

Curriculum Context

The spread of the Apache through North America is one of the biggest migrations of a population group within North America and can be traced in detail.

Apache life. By 1640, the Apache were the first native people to ride horses. Soon afterward, they were also trading the horses to peoples on the Plains.

As white settlers from the east started to move westward, their movement was resisted by the Apache, who had begun raiding settlers in the area after the U.S. government bought New Mexico, the Apache heartland, in 1848. About this time, broken promises and continual intrusion on tribal land led to wars between Native Americans and the U.S. government.

Reservations and resistance

The Apache had their own reasons for going to war. They were angry after a U.S. army attempt in 1861 to seize Cochise, the Chiricahua chief, had resulted in the hanging of six Apache hostages. By 1868, most Apache tribes had been subdued and forced onto reservations. The Chiricahua, with the help of warriors from other Apache groups, continued their raids and attacks until 1872, when Cochise signed a treaty and moved to an Apache reservation in Arizona.

In 1876, the U.S. government attempted to relocate the Apache once again, this time to Alabama. This led to resistance from a breakaway group headed by Geronimo, Cochise's son-in-law. Geronimo—the Mexican nickname for Goyathlay, meaning "the yawner"—inspired terror on both sides of the U.S.–Mexico border with his persistent raiding. Geronimo gave himself up then escaped several times, before finally surrendering in 1886 with his remaining band of fewer than 40 people. They were sent into exile in Florida and then moved to Oklahoma, where Geronimo was confined to Fort Sill and wrote his memoirs. He died in 1909.

A census taken in 2000 showed 57,199 Native Americans claiming Apache descent, many living on reservations in Arizona and New Mexico. With the end of their traditional way of life, a large number of Apache had taken up raising cattle and sheep. Others worked in a range of blue- and white-collar jobs or had become active in tribal enterprise programs.

Family and social life

Up to the mid-19th century, the Apache organized themselves mainly in bands of about 50 extended families. Tribes consisted of between 10 and 20 bands, which would come together in times of crisis or at the annual summer gathering. The bands were completely separate, and alliances were easily made and broken. Each band was led by a chief who emerged as leader by virtue of his bravery and strong personality.

Apache men made weapons, hunted, and went on raids. Women, on the other hand, were in charge of domestic life.

Band

A simple form of human society consisting of an extended kin or family group. Bands are smaller than tribes and have fewer social institutions.

Apache

Language:	Athapascan
Area:	Southwest
Reservation:	Arizona, New Mexico, and Oklahoma
Population:	6,500 Pre-Contact; approximately 50,000 today
Housing:	Mostly tepee and wikiup
European contact:	Francisco de Coronado in 1540
Neighbors:	Pueblo, Zuni, Comanche, and Navajo
Lifestyle:	Nomads and warriors
Food:	Wild plants, small game, and buffalo (Kiowa-Apache)
Crafts:	Basketry and beadwork

One of the last groups to settle in the Southwest, the Apache adapted well to the harsh environment.

Two Apache women watch over a cooking pot on a campfire. This photo was taken around 1903.

They gathered the food, such as mesquite pods, cactus fruits, and piñon nuts, and prepared the meals. They also gathered wood and water, made crafts, and organized the home. Apache women were particularly skilled at basketry, sealing the baskets in pitch so that they could carry liquids in them. Leaks were cured by reheating and smoothing over the pitch. They also used baskets for cooking by coating them in clay.

The Apache lived a partly nomadic existence (moving from place to place), so houses were made from whatever could be found. In the east, they lived in movable buffalo-hide tepees, while in the west they lived in wikiups (dome-shaped brush and grass huts), which were burned when the band moved on.

Tepee

A cone-shaped tent built with a pole framework and traditionally covered with animal skins.

Clothing was originally made from animal skins, including moccasins tied at the knee. By the 1800s, the men wore loose cotton shirts and trousers and headbands in their hair, while women wore full skirts and blouses.

Corn-growing Native Americans and horse-owning white settlers provided opportunities for raids. Raiding was seen as vital for survival and was approved in Apache rituals. The goal was to bring back horses and food for their families. To avoid retaliation, the Apache tended to live in remote highlands and canyons.

The Apache made a sharp distinction between war and raiding. A war party was usually formed to avenge an Apache casualty and was led by a relative of the dead person. Their attitude to warfare contrasted with that of Plains groups—the Apache did not have warrior societies or practice counting coup (touching the enemy in battle with a special stick). Apache youth were taught to be brave but not to die foolishly. In fact, Apache men gained no status from killing and never took scalps in battle.

Rituals and religion

Rituals played a big part in the lives of the Apache. They were usually conducted by a shaman, whose power came through contacts with the spirit world, but individuals also sought help from the spirits when taking on a difficult or dangerous task. Spirits were thought to influence and control everything in the world, thereby reinforcing the Apache view that spirits, humans, and the natural world were all connected.

Shaman
A person with special powers to access the spirit world and an ability to use magic to heal the sick and control events.

Mountain spirits

Among the most important of the supernatural beings that came to the aid of the Apache were the *gans*, or mountain spirits. These were ancient deities whose dance represented the Apache migrations from their original homeland far north in the Subarctic region.

The gans also appeared in a Western Apache girl's puberty ceremony, in which the girl was dressed in white buckskin, which symbolized her innocence and purity, and was said to be filled with the gans' healing power. She was also believed to represent White Painted Woman, a god who gave the Western Apache the original ceremony for marking the change from childhood to womanhood and was associated with growth and fertility. During the four days of the puberty ceremony, people of all ages approached the girl to receive the gans' and White Painted Woman's blessings for good health and a long life.

Athapascan

The Athapascan are hunting and fishing people. Their homeland lies in Alaska, south of the Arctic circle, in forests and hills where the climate is cold and snowy for much of the year. Their way of life was originally nomadic, traveling around in search of food.

Because they were always on the move, the Athapascan spent time decorating their bodies, clothes, and weapons, rather than making objects for the home. For example, they ornamented their clothes with fringes, porcupine quills, beads, and shells.

Making use of natural resources

When a hunter caught an animal, such as a caribou, the meat and fat were eaten, the bones were used as tools and weapons, and the skin was used for clothing and tent covers. The people also used birchbark to make canoes, bowls, and other objects.

In winter, the Athapascan often lived in underground houses or in log houses with sod (turf) roofs. They made a variety of snowshoes for different weather conditions. In summer, they made birchbark houses or built small shelters made of branches and brushwood.

Tribes and ceremonies

The Athapascan believe that their people originated in the Alaskan territory, and this view is expressed in ritual and folklore. Among the most important Athapascan ceremonies are those held in honor of the dead or to celebrate events such as a birth or marriage. The Athapascan have also been influenced by neighboring peoples of the Northwest Coast, with whom they traded, and have taken over customs such as the potlatch. During the potlatch, gifts are distributed as a means of showing respect for deceased members of the group or in honor of distant relatives.

Potlatch

A ceremony common to several Native American societies of the Northwest Coast, in which an important person hosts a feast for guests. Relationships within and between clans and villages are reinforced, and the host demonstrates his wealth and raises his status by giving away gifts.

The Athapascan call themselves *Dine*, or *Dene*, which means "the people," and speak a number of different dialects. Tribal groups include the Ingalik, Koyukon, Tanana, Han, Kutchin, Ahtna, and Tanaina. The Ingalik, Kutchin, and Ahtna all have distinct cultures within the main body of Athapascan culture.

Curriculum Context

The Athapascan language group is a useful example to study when comparing the diversity of languages in Native American societies.

Natural and spiritual

Every group of Athapascan had a leader or sometimes two. One group known as the Chandalar Kutchin had two types of leader: one a successful hunter and trapper and the other a warrior. Another important figure was the shaman (medicine man), who had special powers to control the spirit world for the benefit of the tribe.

There are many stories in Athapascan culture that explain and celebrate their central beliefs. In the past, these stories were not written down but told at

Athapascan

Language:	Athapascan
Area:	Subarctic
Reservation:	No official reservation
Population:	No estimates available
Housing:	Bush shelters and wigwams
European contact:	Hudson's Bay Company traders and French trappers
Neighbors:	Tlingit and Cree
Lifestyle:	Hunting and fishing
Food:	Caribou and small game, fish, berries, nuts, and roots
Crafts:	Porcupine quillwork, barkwork, and some wood carving

The Athapascan, although Subarctic, spoke a language that spread across western North America.

gatherings and other occasions, so the legends were passed on from generation to generation.

Humans, animals, and spirits

The Athapascan continue to believe that human beings and animals have an equal relationship. They do not see humans as superior to or different from animals. Although the Athapascan have hunted and killed animals for food to survive, they believe that animals have a spirit worthy of respect. Some specific animals are considered to have special powers that could be used to harm or benefit people. Many Athapascan also believe in reincarnation: the idea that when a person dies, he or she may come back to life in another form.

The Athapascan way of life is centered on the notion that there is a unity in the human, natural, and spiritual world. Like many other Native Americans, the Athapascan people believe that all the natural elements of the world have a spirit and that everything is connected. The Athapascan teach that if we exploit and mistreat the natural world, we endanger our own way of life.

Confronting prospectors

During the Alaskan Gold Rush (1884–1920), the Athapascan way of life changed dramatically. White prospectors invaded Athapascan territory searching for gold. They brought with them many problems for the Athapascan. These ranged from unfamiliar diseases and new trading practices to competition for land and general resources.

When the gold ran out, most white people left the region and the Athapascan returned to some of their old customs. Today, many Athapascan still depend on hunting and fishing for their livelihood, though some communities have adopted a more Western lifestyle.

Curriculum Context

Many curricula ask students to compare European and Native American attitudes toward nature.

Alaskan Gold Rush

The discovery of gold on the Klondike River near Dawson City in Yukon territory in 1896, there brought a frenzied rush of immigrants to the region. By 1898, there were 40,000 prospectors in the area.

Aztec

The Aztecs were originally mercenary warriors who roamed across northern Mexico. Toward the end of the 12th century, they migrated south to central Mexico, settling mostly around Lake Texcoco.

In 1325, the Aztecs began to build their capital, Tenochtitlán (the site of modern Mexico City), on small swampy islands in Lake Texcoco. The Aztecs were forced into exile on these islands by stronger neighbors. However, legend has it that they chose that site to fulfill a prophesy that said the Aztecs would build a great civilization on the spot where they found an eagle perched on a cactus eating a snake.

Island city

Building on the marshland was very difficult. There were no pack animals or wheeled transport, so the Aztecs brought materials from the mainland using flat-bottomed boats until they built causeways. In all, it took a hundred years to build the city.

The people of Tenochtitlán grew their own food on *chinampas*. These were made by sinking bundles of reeds between poles and piling mud from the lake onto this base.

At its height, the city of Tenochtitlán stretched for 5 square miles (13 sq. km). It was connected to the mainland by four long causeways. A network of canals ran through the city, allowing easy transportation of goods and people.

Tenochtitlán was divided into districts that were occupied by people who shared a trade, but the center of the city was dominated by the main ceremonial complex of temples. On the far side of the city was the main marketplace, where up to 50,000 people would

Chinampas

Rectangular artificial islands of fertile land. Crops and flowers were grown, fertilized by lake sediments and human excrement.

Curriculum Context

Students should analyze how the Aztec empire arose in the 14th and 15th centuries.

gather to barter goods. In the early 16th century, Tenochtitlán was one of the largest cities in the world, with an estimated population of 250,000.

The empire
The Aztecs rose to power serving as mercenaries (soldiers fighting for money) for a neighboring city–state. They conquered it in 1428, taking over its territories. This was the beginning of an empire spanning from central Mexico to Guatemala.

Aztec hierarchy

Aztec society was based on a pyramid-shaped hierarchy. The king was at the top and was responsible for war and foreign affairs. He shared government with the Snake Woman (actually a man), who controlled the city's affairs. Next came the nobility, composed of priests and high-ranking warriors. All young men over the age of 15, except priests, trained as warriors. Nobility was gained through acts of bravery, yet the ultimate honor for a warrior was to be killed in battle. Next came the bureaucrats and tradesmen, then the merchants and commoners. The lowest group of citizens was the peasants. They were landless and worked as tenant farmers for the nobles. Last came slaves—men captured in battle or women sold into bondage.

The Aztecs forced weaker states to supply warriors as a form of tribute (payment) and regularly sent tax collectors to the conquered city-states. These officials were always accompanied by fierce warriors.

Mayan calendar
The Aztecs lived by a complex calendar system developed by the Maya. The Mayan civilization was older than the Aztec, and the Maya had built large pyramid cities in the Yucatán Peninsula. The Mayan calendar combined a sacred year of 260 days used by priests alongside a solar year of 365 days used for daily life. Every 52 years, the two calendars coincided, creating a period that the Aztecs considered dangerous and uncertain. During this period,

Aztec priests would perform special rites and even human sacrifices to please the gods.

Human sacrifice

The Aztecs worshiped many gods, including Huitzilopochtli (sun god), Quetzalcoatl (god of learning and crafts), Coyolxauhqui (moon goddess), and Tlaloc (rain god). They believed that the gods protected them in return for the most valuable thing they could offer—life. Human sacrifice was a central part of Aztec religion. It was so basic that they believed human blood made the sun rise and kept the land fertile. Sacrifice had been practiced for a thousand years, but the Aztecs introduced mass sacrifice to show their greatness and to frighten their rivals. Spanish reports

Human sacrifice
Killing people for ceremonial or religious purposes. A number of early Native American peoples used human sacrifices as offerings to their gods.

Aztec

Language:	Nahuatl
Area:	Central Mexico
Reservation:	Along the Colorado and Gila rivers, 400 acres (162 ha), established in 1912
Population:	20 million in 1519; approximately a million today (constituting the largest native group in Mexico)
Housing:	Thatch (commoners), mud-brick (artisans), and stone (nobles)
European contact:	Hernando Cortés in 1519
Neighbors:	Tupanecs, Chichimecs, and Mixtecs
Lifestyle:	Farmers, traders, and warriors
Food:	Corn, beans, squash, and other vegetables, with meat on special occasions
Crafts:	Featherwork, goldwork, jewelry (using precious stones such as jade and turquoise), textiles, and sculpture

The Aztec Empire dominated central and southern Mexico. When the Spanish arrived, 20 million people lived in the Aztec Empire. Within a hundred years, more than 19 million had been wiped out, mostly by disease.

Curriculum Context

Students should examine the reasons for human sacrifice by the Aztecs when studying Native American religious beliefs.

claimed that the Aztecs could sacrifice thousands of people at a time, but the accounts were probably exaggerated. During the ceremony, a victim was forced onto a special stone and held there by four priests. A fifth priest cut out the victim's still-beating heart with a flint knife and dedicated it to the gods.

The arrival of the Spanish

By the late 15th century, the Aztecs were the dominant force in central and southern Mexico and ruled a loose federation of city–states. They expanded their empire in order to gather tribute (payments of money) and captives for human sacrifice. In 1502, Montezuma II was emperor of 38 provinces with 20 million subjects.

In 1519, a conquistador, Hernando Cortés, and 600 Spanish soldiers under his command landed on the eastern coast of Mexico. Within two years, they had destroyed the mighty empire and enslaved its people. Three factors contributed to the Aztec defeat. One was the clever exploitation of internal divisions within the Aztec Empire by the Spanish. This brought the Spanish many local allies. Another factor was the conquistadors' superior weapons. And finally, Montezuma II's failure to act decisively contributed.

Prophecies and omens

Montezuma II was unsure whether he should regard the Spaniards as hostile or as allies. An Aztec myth prophesied that the god Huitzilopochtli and the banished god Quetzalcoatl would have a confrontation in the year that Cortés arrived. Montezuma II had always claimed he was descended from Quetzalcoatl and thought that Cortés' arrival was now confirming the prophecy. Some historians have suggested that Montezuma II was troubled by several ominous signs leading up to the Spanish arrival, including the appearance of a comet. His suspicions were confirmed after hearing of the Spanish victory at Tlaxcala against a superior army that had successfully resisted the Aztecs for many years.

This is the Sun Stone, or Aztec Calendar, in the National Anthropological Museum in Mexico City. It portrays stories from Aztec legends about the universe and shows how the Aztecs measured time.

Montezuma II welcomed Cortés and his soldiers with gifts and invited them into his city. Once inside the city, Cortés took Montezuma II prisoner and demanded more treasure. The Spanish presence in Tenochtitlán was tolerated for several months, but when the Spaniards sacked the Great Temple, the Aztecs attacked them. Montezuma II was killed during the fighting. The Spanish were besieged in the Great Temple. Realizing their time was up, the Spanish tried to sneak out of the city at night but were caught halfway along a causeway by the pursuing Aztecs. Those who were laden down with loot were killed.

The end of the empire

Set on revenge, Cortés returned in 1521 with Spanish reinforcements and boats, which he brought overland in sections to help him besiege the city. After 75 days, the Aztecs finally surrendered.

The fall of Tenochtitlán did not mark the collapse of the Aztec Empire. However, the Aztec population was reduced from more than 20 million in 1519 to under a million in less than 100 years. Most of the loss was due to people dying from European diseases, such as typhus and smallpox, to which they had no resistance.

Curriculum Context

Spanish interaction with the Aztecs is an important aspect to study when evaluating the wider Spanish relationship with Native Americans.

Beothuk

The Beothuk were a small group of Algonquian-speaking Subarctic Native Americans—thought to have been around 500 strong—who lived on the island of Newfoundland, off the northeast tip of Canada. They hunted caribou and sea mammals, for which they developed a unique birchbark canoe with a V-shaped section and raised gunwales (sides).

L'Anse aux Meadows

The ruins of a Norse settlement built around 1000 CE in northern Newfoundland. The buildings were wooden framed and covered with turf. They included workshops for iron working, carpentry, and boat repair.

Genocide

The destruction of a specific group or race.

When the Norse (ancient Norwegians) founded a colony on Newfoundland at L'Anse aux Meadows about 1000 CE, the Beothuk were the first people with whom they came into contact. Centuries later came English settlers, whose relationship with the Beothuk was one of mutual distrust.

Colonial genocide

The Beothuk were badly treated by all who came in contact with them. In 1501, a Portuguese explorer, Caspar Corte Real, kidnapped 57 Beothuk who were later sold as slaves. There are also records of English and French fishermen shooting Beothuk in reprisal for thefts from their ships. This drove the Beothuk inland, where they could not harvest vital seafood.

By 1800, the Beothuk population was down to only a few hundred, and they then became the victims of colonial genocide. The French introduced scalp-taking as a means of destroying the Beothuk and offered the neighboring Micmac people a bounty for every Beothuk scalp they took.

In 1810, the British governor issued orders for the protection of the Beothuk, but it was already too late. In 1827 an expedition to Newfoundland failed to find a single surviving Beothuk. It is possible, however, that a few Beothuk people found refuge on the mainland with their old trading partners, the Naskapi.

Californian Tribal Groups

The modern-day state of California matches almost exactly a geographical area that was for centuries the home of a collection of Native Americans known as the Californian tribal groups. These groups formed one of the largest populations in the Pre-Contact era, containing as much as 10 percent of the native inhabitants of North America.

The people were separated into an estimated 500 small tribal groups that had a great variety of languages, political and social organization, rituals, and beliefs. The tribal groups developed diverse cultures, due in part to California's varied terrain and weather. The land ranges from dense redwood forests and chaparral scrub to oak parklands. Some of these areas have very heavy rainfall; others suffer drought. Survival meant adapting to these different conditions.

Plentiful food

Most of the Californian microenvironments contained such abundant food resources that there was little incentive for the development of agriculture or farming to supplement hunting and gathering. A main resource was the acorn, which—after removing the poisonous tannins by repeated poundings and washings—was used in making acorn bread, a staple food found throughout much of the area. Elsewhere people were dependent on food from the sea, such as fish and sea mammals. Interior mountain peoples spent much time hunting deer and smaller animals.

A well-developed system of distribution enabled tribes in the interior to exchange furs and meat for products from the coastal groups. This helped avoid any regional shortage of food supplies. To make trading easier, a system of shell-money, or *kaia*, was used in which various lengths of strung shell beads had

Curriculum Context

Californian Native American exploitation of natural resources can be studied when comparing European and Native American economic systems.

predetermined values. Many wealthy families sewed kaia strings to the plaited aprons of the female members of the family, which served as a way for them to display their wealth within the group.

The Californian tribes fall into three main groups: those of the south, the central tribes, and those of the north. They all share Californian traits—such as democratic leadership, highly developed basketry skills, and a hunting–gathering lifestyle—the histories of and influences within each group are distinctive.

Southern tribes
Southern tribal groups were the most adversely affected by outside interference. They were collectively known as Mission Indians because of the establishment of Spanish missions in their homelands. After 1769, the Spanish missions stretched from San Diego in the south to San Francisco in the north. At these missions, members of vastly different groups were indiscriminately thrown together, regardless of whether or not they understood each other's language or shared similar social or religious customs and beliefs.

Many traditional crafts, especially basketry made of coiled grass, rush, and yucca, have been lost, and only remnants of other influences from the Southwest remain, such as the use of sand paintings based on the movements of the stars. Most of these traditions vanished with the undermining of the southern shamans (medicine men) by Spanish priests.

Modern groups with a tribal identity include the Seri of Baja California and the Chumash, San Juan Capistrano, Gabrielino, Nicoleno, Diegueno, and Luiseño.

Central tribes
The central region is thought of as the most typically Californian. Few outside influences and disruptions and

Hunting–gathering
Obtaining food by hunting wild animals and eating plants gathered from the wild.

Curriculum Context

Students might be asked to describe the daily lives of the people who occupied the Spanish missions.

a reluctance to travel away from friends and family ensured that local customs were maintained. Life centered around the family house and the extended family group. These people were well known for their qualities of gentleness, amiability, and stability.

Their leadership was based on civil and military chiefs, with the military chief barred from ever raising a hand in anger. He had to remain neutral and negotiate settlement payments in shell-money if family feuds or rivalries began to get out of hand.

Shamanism was important and linked with a belief that dreams were the basis of all power and knowledge. Village councils, at which important matters were discussed, began by each participant describing recently experienced dreams.

Modern central tribes include the Maidu, the Pomo, the Yuki, Yokuts, and Wintun.

Northern tribes

Tribes in northern California tended to be more aggressive as a result of contact with peoples who lived on the Northwest Coast. Even here, though, war was generally thought of as a bad thing, with feuding restricted to families. There was nevertheless a danger of feuds escalating because of the importance placed on personal status and wealth. This could often lead to an insult being enough to justify a violent response.

Households held ownership rights in stands of oak and timber, as well as to hunting and fishing areas, depending on their status. Plank housing, dugout canoes, and the purchase of shamanic power from one's ancestral group were also local characteristics.

Modern tribes belonging to the northern California groups include the Yurok, Karok, and Hupa.

Extended family
A family that includes grandparents and uncles, aunts, and cousins, rather than just parents and their children.

Dugout canoe
A canoe hollowed out of a tree trunk.

Chinook

The Chinook occupied a number of settlements along the Columbia River in the Pacific Northwest, from the river mouth at Cape Disappointment to beyond the falls and rapids known as the Dalles. Unlike many Native Americans, they did not form tribal groups but lived as small bands who all spoke the same language. Differences in dialect and culture between the settlements of these bands were very small.

Each settlement had one or more principal village. The people moved from these to temporary camps along with the seasons. At the camps, they would hunt, fish, or gather local vegetation for food.

At Shoalwater Bay, the major resource was shellfish, particularly clams and mussels. The peoples living near the Dalles collected large numbers of salmon, which lay exhausted in shallow pools after their swim up the rapids. Today, groups are scattered on several reservations under different names, among them the Clatsop, Wasco, and Wishram.

Trade and the Chinook

The Chinook groups were important not only because of their culture, which was basically of the Northwest Coast tradition, but also because of their unique location. They were able to control trade from Shoalwater Bay and the lower parts of the Columbia River. They also used Coast Salish tribes, Sahaptin tribes of the Plateau, and Shoshoni groups of the northern Great Basin to extend their control of trade.

Chinook trade connections extended from the Dalles to the Northwest Coast, the Great Basin and Plateau, and even across the Rockies to the Great Plains. These trade connections were exploited by Europeans and Americans after 1792, when they began mooring their

Curriculum Context

Students comparing European and Native American systems of trade could usefully study the Chinook trading network.

ships at the mouth of the Columbia River and began trading in fur with the Chinook.

From that date, fur-trading ships began to call regularly at the Columbia River. The crews bought tanned elk hides from the Chinook, which they exchanged farther up the coast for more valuable sea-otter robes. In return, the Chinook received guns, powder and shot, steel knives, axes, and other European goods. The Chinook traded these goods at enormous profit to Native American groups farther inland who had no contact with Europeans.

Chinook jargon

With the Chinook acting as middlemen, the lower Columbia area became the center for the regional fur trade, first with the Northwest Fur Company and then with the Hudson's Bay Company. A trade language known as Chinook Jargon spread rapidly along the coast. It was based on the original native language, from before the fur-trading days, and contained many words of native origin as well as words from French and English. Many native words in the jargon come from Nootkan, but there is no historic record of a direct link between the Chinook and the Nootka. Also it is uncertain how important trade and contact between the groups were in prehistoric times.

Contact with Europeans eventually proved disastrous for the Chinook. In 1805, their population was estimated at 16,000. Fifty years later, when the Oregon Trail opened Chinook areas to white settlement, and the Chinook became scattered in reservations, their population had fallen below 3,000. During the reservation period, disease and other troubles reduced their numbers to under 300.

Oregon Trail

A main migration route from the Mississippi River to Oregon, used between 1841 and 1869 before railroads were built.

When ethnographic work (studies of races and cultures) began in the region toward the turn of the 20th century, the descendants of the Chinook had only a distant memory of their traditional culture.

Chumash

Occupying a region centered on the Santa Barbara Channel off the southern coast of California, the Chumash developed specialized crafts and technological skills that amazed the Spanish when they first settled here in the 18th century.

Carved and polished wood bowls, finely woven baskets, and skillfully constructed plank canoes were only part of the Chumash achievement. They had a flourishing economy and a stable political organization. They settled in large villages, with populations of up to 1,000, that prospered as trading and manufacturing centers. This allowed them to take full advantage of the plentiful and varied resources available in the area.

The Chumash and astronomy

The Chumash had gathered a lot of knowledge about stars and planets, which was interpreted in ritual activities by a powerful group of shaman priests (medicine men). This knowledge was ignored by the Spanish priests, despite the fact that the ideas and observations of the Chumash were at least as advanced as those of European societies. The last ceremony conducted by Chumash priests was in the early 1870s, so historians can no longer obtain this knowledge directly from the Chumash. However, archaeology, history, and astronomy are helping piece together the legacy left by southern Californian peoples.

Part of this legacy can be seen in the numerous painted rock-art shrines that are found all over the Santa Barbara area. These paintings were made by Chumash shaman priests, and they may indicate areas of sacred importance to the Chumash. But it is also clear that many of these rock paintings either refer to gods and heavenly events or may even have some other astronomical significance that has not yet been discovered.

Curriculum Context

The Chumash use of astronomy in their religion can be compared with other Native American religious beliefs and practices.

Coast Salish

The Coast Salish lived in settled villages in Washington State, on Vancouver Island, and on the mainland of British Columbia. They were the most southerly people to belong to mainstream Northwest Coast culture.

Although there was not the extreme personal rivalry as in groups such as the Kwakiutl, Salish headmen were extremely proud of their family ancestry and confirmed important social positions by giving generous gifts.

Despite the importance of status, the Salish did not have many ranked dancing societies with privileged positions, which are common to other Northwest Coast peoples. They frequently asked for spirits' help with hunting and canoe-making. These spirits were divided into different groups—those of the seas, mountains, animals, or of natural events. The Salish made requests to the spirits in winter ceremonies (also known as Spirit Singing or Dramatizations of Dreams) when individuals "danced out" their power before invited audiences.

Tribal communities

In the villages, with several families sharing gabled plank housing—similar to but not as decorated as the houses of other Northwest Coast tribes. Each family had its own fireplace at which food was prepared, although families would share with each other in times of shortage. Salmon was a staple food, eaten fresh in season and dried for use in winter. The Coast Salish also ate a variety of other foods, including eggs, roots, berries, and bulbs.

Modern Salish communities have developed crafts that appeal to a nonnative market. The main craft is the weaving of jackets and sweaters from homespun wool with traditional designs. They are based on knitting techniques adopted from early Scottish traders.

Plank housing

Housing of the Northwest Coast peoples, made from the cedar tree. Vertical cedar logs are clad with planks harvested from still-living trees. The planks are tied to the logs with cedar ropes and can be taken down and carried on seasonal migrations. The roof is also made of cedar wood.

Haida

The Haida are people of the Northwest Coast. They live on the Queen Charlotte Islands in Canada's most westerly province, British Columbia, and on Prince of Wales Island in southwest Alaska. They speak Haida, one of the 22 Na-Dené languages (a group of related Native American languages that also includes the Tlingit and Athapascan speakers).

The name *Haida* was given to these people by early European visitors to the area. Today, some Canadian Haida prefer to be called by a traditional clan name, *Xaadas*. The Alaskan Haida are known as *Kaigani*.

In the past, the Haida were renowned for their war exploits and skills at canoeing. Today, they are mainly associated with magnificently carved wooden sculptures and beautiful textiles.

Lifestyle of the Haida

Haida society was organized into two main tribal divisions, or moieties, called Eagles and Ravens. Members of each group lived in separate areas of a village and chose a spouse from the other group. Each moiety was further subdivided into smaller clans.

Fishing and hunting provided the Haida with the staple foods of their diet: fish—particularly salmon and cod—and meat. The tribe also gathered fruit, berries, and nuts from the forest. The greatest of the Haida feasts was the potlatch, which could last for up to 10 days. The potlatch was held to mark the social and political status of a tribe member or to celebrate events such as the raising of a totem pole.

Yellow and red cedar trees were the Haida's most useful resources. The Haida were skilled carpenters and carvers, and after trading began with Europeans in the

Moiety

One of two groups into which many Native American tribes were divided. Each was often composed of related clans, and marriage to someone of the same moiety was usually forbidden.

Totem pole

Sculptures carved from large trees by tribes of the Northwest Coast. The designs illustrate legends or important events, clan lineages, or shamanic powers.

late 18th century, they had access to iron tools. These tools enabled them to carve even more elaborate totem poles, houses, and canoes. Their dugout canoes were made from giant cedar logs. The Haida also used these logs to build their long plank houses and to carve their totem poles.

Haida longhouses

The Haida's longhouses were large, with several rooms. Each house accommodated a number of families, and up to 40 people might be sharing the living space. At the front of the house, there was usually a portal pole, with an opening at the bottom allowing entry into the house. Other carved poles at the front supported the roof beams. The Haida carved memorial poles representing a family emblem or crest, which often exceeded 50 feet (15 m) in height. The dead were sometimes buried in mortuary poles that were put up in graveyards.

The present
Many Haida died as a result of diseases, especially smallpox, which were brought into the region by Europeans toward the end of the 18th century. Those who survived in the Queen Charlotte Islands gathered together in two villages, one at Skidegate and the other at Masset. In Alaska, the Haida congregated in five villages, which have now been reduced to one multiclan village at Hydaburg.

The Haida and other Northwest Coast peoples carved totem poles from cedar. This one has carvings of a hawk moon and an eagle.

Hohokam

The Hohokam people lived in a region centered on the dry desert lands of the Gila and Salt River valleys, in present-day Arizona, from about 300 BCE until the mid-1400s CE. They were one of the three main prehistoric groups in the Southwest, the others being the Mogollon and the Anasazi.

Curriculum Context

The Hohokam are an interesting example of early urban dwellers in the Americas.

Kiva

An underground structure used for communal gathering, ceremonies, and councils, that is typical of early Anasazi settlements.

Platform mound

An earthwork created to support a structure or an activity.

Peaceful farmers, the Hohokam dug a large-scale and efficient network of irrigation canals. It allowed them to grow corn, beans, squash, and cotton in the usually barren desert beyond the fertile floodplains. The network of canals totaled over 600 miles (965 km), watered more than 200,000 acres (80,000 ha), and may have supported some 60,000 people.

The Hohokam lived in large villages and towns: Snaketown, the main Hohokam settlement, covers more than 300 acres (120 ha) and contains the ruins of more than 100 kivas.

The Hohokam disappeared abruptly about 1450. Their descendants may be the Papago and Pima peoples, who still live in the area: *Hohokam* is a Pima word meaning "the vanished ones."

Archaeological finds

It appears that the Hohokam traded regularly with people in Mesoamerica. Evidence for this at Hohokam are the remains of ball courts, well-developed platform mounds, and items such as clay figurines, mirrors made from iron pyrites, and copper bells.

It also seems that many Hohokam villages had mixed populations, with people from other groups living in them. Many sites contain the remains of pottery that is a mixture of Hohokam and other styles. Also there is great variety in the types of kivas at many sites.

Hopi

The Hopi occupy about a dozen villages in northeastern Arizona. They are the westernmost of the Pueblo peoples, and their territory is surrounded on all sides by the Navajo reservation. The name *Hopi* is derived from their own name for themselves, "the peaceful ones." The Hopi are descended from people who migrated into the Southwest before 1000 BCE.

Mesa villages

Since ancient times, Hopi communities have built on a high plateau known as Black Mesa. These mesa-top villages provided protection from enemies, while the land below was used to grow corn, beans, squash, cotton, and other crops. They also hunted and ate wild foods such as pine nuts, prickly pear, and seeds.

Domesticated animals were introduced in the 16th century, and the Hopi began raising sheep, cattle, horses, and *burros*. Fruit trees were imported by the Spanish, as were melons, wheat, and chilies.

Burro
A small donkey used as a pack animal.

The Hopi first encountered Europeans in 1540, when the Spanish explorer Francisco de Coronado sent a small party to explore their region. Later, mission stations were founded in five communities. In 1680, the Hopi joined the Pueblo Rebellion, and the Spanish presence temporarily ended. When they returned 12 years later, the Spanish had little impact on the Hopi.

Mission stations
Religious outposts established by Spanish Roman Catholic priests to convert the indigenous people to Christianity.

During the 18th and early 19th centuries, the Hopi suffered from raids by Mexicans, Apache, and Navajo. The United States took control of the Southwest after 1848, and, in 1850, the Hopi asked for U.S. protection from Navajo attacks. In the following years, contact with white people increased. Several Protestant and Mormon missions were established after 1870. In 1882, the Hopi were assigned a reservation. However, the allocation of land caused internal strife; factions within villages separated and formed new communities.

Conflict and continuity

During the 20th century, the Navajo, with their livestock, began to take Hopi lands set aside for use by both groups. This brought the Hopi and Navajo into conflict and resulted in several lawsuits.

Today, some Hopi still farm their ancestral lands, while others work for wages and many families also sell craft items. Popular Hopi handicrafts include decorated pottery, silverwork, basketry items, and carved kachina dolls. Men also weave wool and cotton cloth for use in ceremonial garments.

While each Hopi village has a unique ceremonial life, religious activity follows a common pattern. Each year, a series of ancient stories is reenacted in the belief that their faithful retelling ensures harmony in the universe. In various ceremonies between midwinter and midsummer, dancers are masked and wear costumes to represent kachinas. Other ceremonies are associated with harvest time, men's and women's societies, and the winter solstice.

Kachina dolls
Carved dolls that represent spirit beings (kachinas), given to children to educate them.

The Snake and Antelope ceremony is the best known of the Hopi ceremonies. On the ninth day of this rite, men dance in the village plaza with live snakes in their mouths which are then released at sacred sites far from the village. This historic photo shows priests chanting during the ceremony.

Hupa

The Hupa come from northwestern California. They originally lived in small villages along the Trinity River in the Hoopa Valley, from which their name was derived. Today, the Hupa live on a U.S. government reservation in the same region. Their language is Athapascan.

In the past, the Hupa lived in plank houses and ate wild plant foods, such as nuts and seeds. They fished for salmon and sturgeon from the Trinity River and hunted deer in the forests. They also grew tobacco.

Food and wealth

The Hupa had a very structured society, with a chief at the top. Their social system was based on wealth, although the richest man in a village was not always the chief. Wealthy members of the tribe were allowed to enslave other members who were in debt to them.

Hupa who grew rich did so through the ownership and exclusive use of hunting areas, fishing sites, and groves of oak trees, from which acorns were harvested. The Hupa used the shells of sea mollusks as money. Shell necklaces were worn as a sign of a person's wealth.

Villages were formed by groups sharing the same family line. Each village was responsible for its own law and order, since Hupa customs and beliefs varied widely, although the people spoke the same language.

Before 1848, the Hupa were completely isolated. However, when the Hoopa Valley was overrun by prospectors during the California gold rush in the 1850s, the tribe was driven from its homelands.

Today, the Hupa have lost much of their way of life. Their current population is fewer than 500.

Curriculum Context

Some curricula may ask students to compare differences between European and Native American attitudes toward property, land ownership, and other economic ideas.

Inuit

The Inuit live in the Arctic region, which extends from Siberia, across northern Canada, to Greenland. Their language, Eskimo-Aleut, is unrelated to any other, and their tribal name *Inuit* simply means "the people."

Although they live in such a vast area, Inuit speakers from Greenland and Siberia are able to understand one another's dialects. The Inuit were formerly called Eskimos, a name that comes from the Algonquian-speaking groups to the south of their region. It means "raw meat eaters" and was originally meant as an insult.

Bridging continents

The Inuit probably came to North America from Siberia by crossing the Bering Strait about 3000 BCE, when the strait was a land bridge because of low sea levels caused by a recent ice age. Until 1867, when the United States bought Alaska from Russia, Inuit families from North America and Asia often set up winter camps together.

Together with the Aleut, who speak an Inuit dialect, the Inuit are thought to be a different genetic group from other Native Americans. They are physically shorter and broader, and have a distinctive fold of skin on the eyelid that is characteristic of people of Asiatic origin.

Inuit way of life

Only the Central, or Canadian, Inuit lived in igloos, which they made in winter by cutting blocks of frozen snow and building them into a dome shape. A block of stretched walrus gut acted as a window to let in light. People usually entered the igloo by crawling on their hands and knees along a passageway that was built partly below ground level to avoid heat loss from the inside. Inside, there was a raised platform around the sides of the igloo that was covered in furs to serve as

Curriculum Context

Students should be able to show how geological and archaeological evidence explains the origins and migration of peoples from Asia to the Americas.

Igloo

A shelter made of blocks of snow, usually in the form of a dome. They are built by Inuit in the Canadian central Arctic and in Greenland. The smallest are temporary shelters used on hunting trips. Larger ones are semipermanent, one-roomed family homes.

seating and sleeping space. For lighting and cooking, the Inuit used seal-oil lamps.

The Alaskan and Greenland Inuit made their houses from stones, earth, and driftwood. If they lived near the coast and found beached whales, they often used whale ribs to make the foundations of their houses.

Inuit life depended very much on the animals that lived nearby. In Canada and Alaska, there were vast herds of caribou, whereas coastal groups depended more on hunting sea mammals, such as whales, seals, and walruses. These provided food, clothing, materials for weapons, and also skins for making summer tents.

In winter, hunters would look for the seals' breathing holes in the ice and wait there to catch them. In summer, seals, sea lions, and walruses sunned themselves on the ice floes, and Inuit hunters would crawl up behind them and harpoon them.

Today, igloos are only built by hunters as temporary shelters. This photo from around 1924 shows a family constructing an igloo from blocks of snow.

Inuit

Language:	Eskimo–Aleut
Area:	Arctic and Subarctic
Reservation:	None
Population:	127,000 today
Housing:	Igloo, stone, and wood huts
European contact:	18th-century Danish missionaries and European whaling ships
Neighbors:	Chukchi
Lifestyle:	Settled hunters and fishermen
Food:	Fish, seals, walruses, and caribou
Crafts:	Ivory carving and boatbuilding

The Inuit people are scattered over a very large area.

Curriculum Context

The Inuit provide an interesting example of how Native Americans exploit natural resources.

Inuit clothing

The Inuit made their clothes from the animals they caught. The inland groups wore coats, leggings, mittens, stockings, and boots made from caribou skin, with the fur worn next to the skin in winter for added warmth. Coastal groups relied more on sea mammals. They made wind- and waterproof parkas from seal intestines and feather coats from the many migratory birds the Arctic attracts. They also generally wore several layers of clothing; each layer trapped warm air and prevented damp from reaching the wearer.

Inuit clothing was usually decorated with patterns, fringes, buttons, and embroidery. Some of this was very practical: a wolf-fur fringe around the hood of a parka helped protect the wearer from frostbite. They also wore snow goggles to protect their eyes from the dazzling effects of sunlight on summer snow and sewed all their clothes so that the stitches never penetrated the outside of the garment, where holes would allow damp to enter. Earrings, nose-rings, ivory or wooden lip-plugs, and tattooing were also among Inuit forms of personal adornment.

For travel over water, the coastal Inuit used kayaks. They also used larger boats called *umiaks* for whaling and trading expeditions. Inland, the Inuit traveled over snow and ice on sleds pulled by teams of huskies.

Family life

Inuit households included all immediate relatives. In winter, a whole family would live in a one-room home. There were villages but no village leaders. Instead, there were partnerships with other families. The men had "sharing partners" with whom they divided the food they caught. Both men and women also had "name partners," people of the same name from another family with whom they shared gifts.

Kayak

A small boat used by Native Americans in Arctic regions to hunt on lakes, rivers, and in coastal waters. It was traditionally made from a driftwood frame covered with stitched animal skins.

Inupiaq—the Inuit language

Inupiaq has a rich spoken tradition, and the first book in Inupiaq was published in Greenland in 1742. The Inupiaq language is polysynthetic, which means that it has a large number of suffixes, or endings, that can be added to a small number of root words to create verbs, phrases, and even a whole sentence. A root word such as "snow" or "seal" can be altered to give it a very special meaning. The Inuit are famous for their "song duels," in which the two singers or groups of singers trade insults and offensive remarks.

For entertainment, the Inuit told stories and played games. Many Inuit games also had a practical purpose, such as throwing a hunter into the air from a "trampoline" to see distant animals.

The Inuit worshiped the spirits of animals and the forces of nature. Their shamans (religious leaders) helped them understand the relationship between

Northwest Passage
A sea route along the northern coast of North America, connecting the Atlantic and Pacific oceans. Explorers searched for it for centuries as a possible trade route to Asia, but it was not navigated until 1906.

In a modern Inuit settlement on the shore of the Arctic, caribou meat hangs in slices on a rack to dry in the sun.

the human and animal worlds through ceremonies in which the whole community became involved.

The Inuit make miniature ivory carvings of animals and humans. In the past, these were made as good-luck charms, but many Inuit now sell them to tourists.

Contact with Europeans

The first European explorers to encounter the Inuit were the Vikings, led by Eric the Red in 984 CE. He tried to kidnap the women. In the 16th century, an English explorer called Martin Frobisher sailed to the Arctic in search of the Northwest Passage, a hoped-for route to East Asia. Frobisher tried to kidnap one of the Inuit, then returned and kidnapped a family. He put them in a cage to see if they would mate.

Different forms of mistreatment continue today. In Alaska, the Inuit face a huge influx of people working in the oil industry. In 1971, the U.S. government passed an act to protect Inuit lands and grant them funds, but the Inuit see this as an empty gesture and feel the government does not address their real needs.

Kiowa

The Kiowa, who spoke Aztec–Tanoan, lived in the southern Plains. They were among the last Native American groups forced onto a tribal reservation. The Kiowa, whose name means "principal people," was made up of six bands (just five remain today) totaling approximately 1,500 people, plus their allies, the Kiowa–Apache, who spoke an Athapascan language.

The Kiowa migrated into the Plains from the headwaters of the Missouri River about 1700 and allied with the Crow to fight the Arapaho, Sioux, and Cheyenne for control of territory. Even so, by the time Meriwether Lewis and William Clark explored the area in 1805, the Kiowa had been pushed south, where they had been fighting against the Comanche. The Comanche had been, in turn, pushed south across the Arkansas River.

Curriculum Context

Competition for land is an important factor in the spread of native peoples across North America.

Kiowa allies

The Kiowa were highly respected as warriors. In the late 18th century, they maintained friendly trade relations with the people of Taos Pueblo and, in 1790, negotiated a peace settlement with the Comanche. In the early 18th century, the Kiowa fought the Arapaho but made peace after a decisive victory in 1840. Thereafter, the Kiowa, Comanche, and Arapaho became firm allies and they frequently made winter camps together.

War and raiding

War and raiding were a central feature of the Kiowa way of life. Warrior societies were prominent, and martial exploits, acts of bravery, and daring were the principal means by which men won status and honor. The act of counting coup—harmlessly striking or touching one's enemy in battle—was an aspect of warfare that was unknown to Europeans.

Counting coup

Among Plains peoples, an act of bravery in battle involving striking a blow against an enemy warrior's body with a decorated stick. The acts were recorded by making notches in the coup stick or by adding a feather to the warrior's headdress.

Following their alliance with the Comanche, the Kiowa and Crow raided for horses together in Mexico. They became very wealthy because of their horse stocks. The horse featured prominently in their lifestyle, and children were accomplished riders by ages five or six.

The buffalo

The Kiowa lived a similar lifestyle to that practiced by other nomadic (wandering) horsemen of the Plains. They did not plant or harvest food. Instead, their lives were built around the buffalo hunt, living in easily transported tepees. Chief Satanta was typical of many Plains Indians in not understanding why white buffalo hunters took the skins and left the carcasses to rot. He complained to them that "This country is old, but you are cutting down the timber, and now the country is of no account at all." It is estimated that, of nearly four million buffalo killed between 1872 and 1874, only 150,000 were killed by Native Americans.

Kiowa

Language:	Aztec–Tanoan
Area:	Colorado and Oklahoma
Reservation:	Assigned in southwest Oklahoma but lost in 1901
Population:	2,000 in 1800; approximately 10,000 today
Housing:	Three-pole tepees
European contact:	Lewis and Clark in early 19th century
Neighbors:	Comanche, Osage, and Arapaho
Lifestyle:	Nomadic buffalo hunters
Food:	Buffalo and game
Crafts:	Calendric skins and beadwork

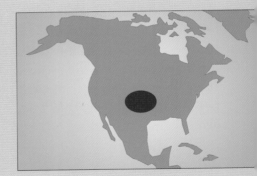

The origins of the Kiowa are unknown, but they may have originated in the Arizona region.

Warrior chiefs

The Kiowa were warrior-horsemen of great skill, led by important chiefs such as Satank (or Sitting Bear), the warlike Lone Wolf, Satanta (or White Bear), and Kicking Bird, who wanted to be on good terms with the whites.

Satanta in particular was an extraordinary figure. He was a large, muscular man who lived in a bright red lodge decorated with red streamers.

On the warpath, he painted his entire body red then rode off, possibly on a red pony, and certainly carrying a red shield. He was honored by the people and feared for his daring. Satanta summed up the feelings of the traditionalists when he declared: "I don't want to settle. I love to roam over the prairies. There I feel free and happy, but when we settle down, we grow pale and die."

Arts and beliefs

The Kiowa also had a rich artistic tradition. Twice a year in summer and winter camp, they recorded major events by painting narrative scenes on animal skins.

They adopted the Sun Dance, as did other Plains tribes, but the Kiowa did not practice self-mutilation and were known to abandon the ceremony if blood was shed accidentally. The Kiowa believed in the power of dreams and visions to endow the individual with supernatural abilities in war, hunting, and healing.

Together with their Comanche allies—whom many Kiowa fought alongside under their famous chief Quanah Parker—the Kiowa spread the peyote religion, centered around the hallucinogenic cactus. Parker's and Lone Wolf's groups were the last Native Americans to roam freely on the southern Plains. Together, these allies have shared territory in Oklahoma since 1868.

Sun Dance

An important ceremony practiced by Native Americans of the Plains to celebrate the renewal of nature.

Peyote

The hallucinogenic peyote cactus of Texas and Mexico has been used in religious ceremonies and for healing by Native Americans for more than 2,000 years. Members of the Native American Church use it today in their religious practices.

Klamath

The Klamath belong to the group of peoples known as the Plateau Indians, who take their name from the Columbia Plateau. The Columbia River, one of the largest in North America, flows through this northwest region.

The Klamath homelands were in the Great Basin of southern Oregon and northern California, near the Upper Klamath Lake and the Klamath River. The Klamath call themselves *Maklaks*, meaning "people," or "community." They are part of the Lutuamian-speaking family of Native Americans. In early days, the Klamath traded with many other peoples in the region who spoke dialects of Lutuamian.

Until the 19th century, the Klamath lived in two types of house. They moved around according to the seasons in search of food. In winter, they built earth-covered houses alongside the many rivers of the Plateau. The houses were half-underground, and this, along with the earth, provided insulation to keep them warm. In the summer, they built temporary lodges of wooden frames covered with bullrush matting.

Food sources

There is a lot of rainfall in the Plateau area, supplying water to the many rivers and streams. The Klamath's main source of food was fish, especially salmon. At the time of year when the salmon swim upriver from the sea to spawn, the Klamath were able to catch many fish using dugout canoes hollowed out from treetrunks.

Throughout the rest of the year, the Klamath hunted elk, deer, and bear at the edge of the forests, as well as antelope and jackrabbits on the plains. They also gathered wild plants on the grasslands. These included roots and bulbs from the camas plant—a kind of lily—water-lily seeds, bitterroot, wild carrots, and wild

Curriculum Context

Many curricula ask students to compare housing and shelter across Native American societies.

onions. The Klamath also ate baked grasshoppers, which were considered a delicacy, and gathered blackberries and huckleberries in the river valleys.

Changing lives

The Klamath were a warlike people who often raided other northern Californian tribes, taking captives to sell as slaves. They were usually friendly to Europeans. In 1829, they established trade relations with a Canadian explorer for the Hudson's Bay Company, Peter Skene Ogden. From then on, they were mainly on peaceful terms with white settlers.

Hudson's Bay Company

A trading company set up in 1670 in the Hudson Bay area of North America. It controlled the fur trade in the region for centuries, forming a network of trading posts and obtaining fur from local Native Americans in exchange for goods shipped from Britain.

In 1864, the Klamath signed a treaty with the government in which they were granted a reservation in Oregon. However, by the terms of the treaty they lost much of their homelands and had to share their reservation with 35 other groups, including their former neighbors, the Modoc.

On the reservation, there was tension between the Klamath and Modoc, largely because there was not enough food, and tribe members became ill. The Modoc rebelled against their treatment by the government, leading to a violent war. The Klamath lost more of their lands when, in 1954, the federal government terminated the tribe's rights to retain its lands on the reservations.

In a photo taken in the 1920s, a Klamath woman kneels as she prepares *wokas* (water lily seeds) on a stone slab. Wokas were one of the main traditional foods of the Klamath people.

Kwakiutl

The Kwakiutl belong to a group of tribes who speak the same language living on the east coast of Vancouver Island and on the mainland in British Columbia. The tribe consists of some 20 village groups who are related by a common language, Wakashan, the main dialect of which is Kwak' wala. Today the Kwakiutl prefer to be known by the name *Kwakwa ka' wakw*, meaning "those who speak Kwak' wala."

Coastal lifestyle

Like other tribal groups of the Northwest Coast, the Kwakiutl traditionally lived in villages set in the narrow strips of land between the water's edge and the region's dense and often impenetrable forests.

Up to 500 people lived in the permanent villages. The traditional type of house was a multifamily house made from cedar planking. More temporary shelters were put up at the tribe's summer camps. Seafood, such as shellfish, crabs, seals, and five species of Pacific salmon, dominated the Kwakiutl diet. The salmon were caught with traps, weirs, harpoons, and nets, and provided a valuable source of protein. Different species of salmon were available at different times of the year, providing the Kwakiutl with fish from spring until December.

Curriculum Context

Movement from one place to another in search of food is a common element of many Native American societies.

The Kwakiutl moved from one site to another within their territory as the seasons changed and different, seasonal food sources became available. Much of the traveling was by water in canoes varying from small, two-passenger canoes to some capable of holding as many as 50 people.

The social order

Other than the family, the basic social unit of the Kwakiutl is the *namima*, consisting of an extended family group, the members of which were descended from a single mythic (imaginary) ancestor, such as the Thunderbird. Several families make up a namima, with several namima making up the village. Each namima had a specific rank within the tribe, as did each individual: first-ranking, second-ranking, and so on in descending order.

Rank was determined mainly by the inheritance of names and privileges—for example, the right to sing certain songs. Potlatches (gift-giving events) were held to confirm the individual's position.

European contact

The first contact the Kwakiutl had with Europeans was most probably with Captain Vancouver and his crew when, in 1792, the captain sailed around the island that now bears his name. However, there had been contact with European goods before this in the form of such objects as French pewterware and Spanish muskets, probably acquired through trade with the Nootka people.

Contact with the Europeans also brought the inevitable diseases to which the native peoples lacked resistance. Tuberculosis and sexually transmitted disease killed many but, in 1862, smallpox killed one-third of the native population of British Columbia. Alcohol, guns, and gunpowder also claimed many native lives in the 19th century.

The present

In common with other Northwest Coast groups, many of the Kwakiutl still live on the lands that were set aside for them by government agencies in the 1860s. With the loss of their traditional way of life, they have learned to adjust to the Canadian economy. Today, many Kwakiutl are employed in the salmon-canning industry, in fishing, construction, and the lumber trade.

Thunderbird

A legendary creature in many Northwest Coast cultures, which creates storms, lightning, and thunder as it flies and which must be prevented from becoming angry.

Curriculum Context

The way the Northwest Coast peoples live today is a legacy of 19th-century federal Indian policy.

Maya

The Mayan civilization began as early as 1500 BCE but declined long before Columbus arrived in the Americas in the late 15th century. It was a sophisticated civilization with beautiful architecture and artifacts, and advanced systems of astronomy and mathematics. Mayan glyphs, or picture-writings, tell scholars about the complex political and religious structure of Mayan society and how the empire rose and fell.

The Maya lived on the Yucatán Peninsula in Mexico and in neighboring areas. Their civilization extended to neighboring peoples, such as the Huastec and the Quiche. These peoples all lived in an area that scholars now refer to as Mesoamerica—parts of present-day Mexico, Guatemala, Belize, Honduras, and Nicaragua.

Olmec inheritance

The Maya were descended from an earlier civilization, the Olmec. The Olmec are known today as the mother civilization of Mesoamerica. They are thought to have invented a system of writing and to have been among the first people to cultivate corn, a crop that they developed over many centuries from wild grass seeds. The Mayan civilization was the greatest to emerge after the Olmec.

Cities of stone

The Maya had a staple diet of corn but also grew crops that were unknown outside the Americas, such as tomatoes, chili peppers, pumpkins, avocados, peanuts, and beans. Because of their plentiful supply of food, the Maya were able to spend time building great cities, which became centers of culture, learning, commerce, and religious ceremonies. There were more than 100 of these Maya cities in Mesoamerica, each full of magnificent stone buildings, such as pyramids with temples on top, palaces, and vaulted tombs. The

Pyramid

A building with triangular outer surfaces that converge to a point. Mesoamericam pyramids are usually stepped with temples at the top.

cities also had bridges, paved roads, bathhouses, courts for ball games, and squares.

Social divisions

Each city was like a state, with its own ruler. The citizens were divided into three social classes. First were the priests, who were called the Keepers of Knowledge. Next were the Sun Children, who administered taxes, commerce, and the law. Then came craftworkers such as potters, stoneworkers, and tailors. In the countryside around the cities lived the farmers, who usually had small, one-roomed houses made of adobe (bricks of straw and clay) and thatch— much like the houses their descendants live in today.

Curriculum Context

Studying the Maya system of agricultural production and trade allows students to explain the rise of city-states.

This step pyramid at Chitchén Itzá was a temple to the god Kukulkan. The Maya designed it so that during the spring and fall equinoxes, the corner of the pyramid and stone serpent head carvings cast a shadow that looks like a huge serpent coming down the pyramid.

The Maya were skilled spinners and weavers, and also made fine pottery and silver, copper, shell, and feather jewelry. It seems that they did not use wheeled vehicles or metal tools.

Main Mayan cities

During the Classic period, from about 300 to 900 CE, Mayan civilization spread over a population of some 10 million. Great cities, such as Tikal, Uxmal, Becan, Chitchén Itzá, and Seibal, were built, and they became independent Mayan kingdom-states.

The greatest city was Palenque, known as the jewel of the Mayan world. In 1952, an archaeologist named Alberto Ruz found a huge tomb at the site of Palenque. Inside was a crypt that had been sealed for over 1,200 years. It contained the sarcophagus, or stone coffin, of Palenque's most powerful ruler, Lord Pacal, whose name means Great Shield. Above Lord Pacal's head was a life-sized jade mask.

Deciphering glyphs

Not long after this great find, archeologists discovered how to decipher the glyphs carved on the coffin. For many years they had been trying to work out the meanings of glyphs inscribed on Mayan buildings and tombs. They had also found books, which were folded sheets of paper made from plant fibers. Finally, they worked out a series of codes that told them a great deal about Mayan civilization.

From the books, archaeologists learned about topics such as agriculture, weather, medicine, and astronomy. They also found that the Maya had used a highly accurate calendar.

Mayan gods

From Lord Pacal's coffin, archaeologists found out that Mayan rulers had their pyramids built for them during

Glyph

A carved or inscribed symbol, which can be a picture, an idea, or part of a writing system.

Curriculum Context

Mayan art and architecture help students understand the Maya cosmic world view.

This small temple at Chitchén Itzá is completely covered with decorations, including masks of the rain god Chac, which stand out at the corners of the building. The figures between the masks include an armadillo, a snail, a turtle, and a crab. In Mayan mythology, these four animals hold up the sky.

their lifetimes, so that people could remember and worship them immediately after their deaths. This meant that the rulers thought of themselves as gods.

The archaeologists also discovered that the Maya worshiped many gods of nature. One of the most important was Chac, the god of rain. The Maya practiced many rituals to make sure that Chac sent them plenty of rain for their crops. There was also a creator god, Kukulcan—who was similar to the Aztec god Quetzalcoatl—and Itzamina, a god of the sky. The

Quetzalcoatl

The creator god of the Toltecs, and later one of the main Aztec gods. He took the form of a feathered serpent.

Violent society

One of the most interesting discoveries that archaeologists have made at Palenque is that, far from being a peaceful people, as was once thought, the Maya were actually violent and aggressive. The Maya placed great value on the military conquest of other peoples and often performed cruel human sacrifices to their gods. In addition, they held ball games on special courts in which the players had to compete for their lives. The losers were sacrificed to the gods.

Maya put complete trust in these gods, whom they believed controlled all aspects of their destiny.

Mayan decline

Nobody knows for sure what caused the decline of the Mayan civilization. Some scholars believe it was a combination of civil war and natural disasters such as drought. For hundreds of years after their decline, the Mayan cities lay hidden in the jungle, until they were uncovered by Spanish explorers in the 16th century. Over the next few centuries, the Spanish conquered most of the remaining Mayan people. But it was not until the early 1800s that the Mexican government subdued the last independent Mayan communities.

Neglected people

During the 19th century, archaeologists became very interested in the relics of Mayan civilization. However, there was less interest in the living descendants of the Maya. Today, the few remaining Maya are mostly poor peasant farmers in Mexico, Guatemala, and Belize. They speak Mayan dialects and make traditional Mayan pottery and sculpture.

Sculptures of rattlesnakes adorn this building at Uxmal. This city of around 25,000 people flourished in the ninth century CE.

Mission Indians

Mission Indians were Native Americans who, from about the 1750s to the middle of the 19th century, were forced to live in missions—settlements built around fortified Christian churches. There were Mission Indians in various parts of North America, but the term is most often applied specifically to native peoples in California who came under the control of Catholic missionaries from Spain in the 18th century.

After 1492, the Spanish worked their way through the West Indies and Central and South America, subduing the native inhabitants and taking over their lands. By the middle of the 18th century, they had begun to establish the first church-run missions.

Native Americans in California

At that time, there were more than 300,000 Native Americans living in California. These people lived in peaceful and settled local communities of very small villages made up of a few related families. Most were hunter–gatherers, whose staple diet was acorns, which they ground up into soup or bread-meal. They hunted rabbit, deer, and quail, fished for salmon, and gathered wild foods such as ryegrass seeds, camas roots, plums, grapes, and manzanita berries.

Hunter–gatherers

People who obtain most of their food by hunting wild animals and eating plants gathered from the wild.

To the Spanish, all Native Americans were heathens whose souls could be saved only by conversion to the Christian faith. The most efficient way to do this was to gather the small tribes into large groups for instruction by priests. The Spanish herded local people together in the missions, regardless of their different tribal identities and of the fact that they spoke different languages. Often we no longer know their original identities—for example, the Fernandeno people were simply all those different people brought together in the mission at San Fernando.

Curriculum Context

Understanding Native Americans and Spanish religious beliefs is important when comparing the interactions between these people in California.

Curriculum Context

Students should be able to identify missionary attitudes and policies toward Native Americans.

Forced into slavery

The Spanish arrived in California in 1769, and Franciscan missionaries enlisted the help of the Spanish army in rounding up the local people and forcing them to work on the missions. In total, Franciscan priests established 21 missions along the California coast, from San Diego to San Francisco.

Forced labor

The declared aim of the missions was to teach the Native Americans Christianity. In reality, the people on the land served as an army of forced farm laborers for the Europeans, and the missions were barracks rather than churches. If the Native Americans tried to escape, they were whipped with barbed lashes or put into solitary confinement without water. Sometimes they were branded, tortured, or even executed. They were given Spanish names, made to wear uniforms, and forced to worship as Catholics. They were given poor shelter, sanitation, and food, and family members were separated. Many died from diseases such as smallpox or from the brutal punishments meted out to them.

Tribes unite in revolt

In 1775, the Ipai and Tipai united to burn down the mission at San Diego. The rebellion took the Spanish a year to put down. Ten years later, a Native American medicine woman, or shaman, named Toypurina led a failed attempt to destroy the San Gabriel mission east of Los Angeles. During the 18th century, there were many revolts, most notably by the Chumash. Many Chumash rebels were later rounded up and returned to their missions, while others were executed or sentenced to forced labor in chain-gangs.

During the 19th century, the Mexican government ended the church's right to imprison Native American people against their will. However, this created new problems for the Mission Indians. Their villages were gone, and many of them starved when the missions closed or were turned into ranches. Some remained

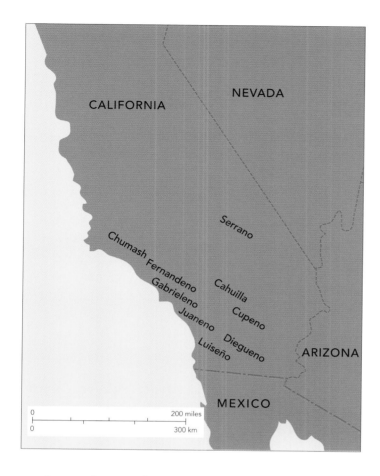

This map shows the locations of the main Californian Mission Indians. The original tribal identities of many Mission Indians are no longer known. The name *Luiseño*, for example, refers to all the people who were gathered together in the mission at San Luis.

on the ranches, working as poor laborers. In 1848, the United States took control of California from the Mexicans, and the California gold rush started. Former Native American lands were now settled by white immigrants.

Too little, too late

By the late 19th century, the U.S. government finally began to establish reservation lands for the Native Americans, but by then most of the former native homelands were owned by whites and the Native American population had been decimated. By 1900, there were only 10,000 left. In the 20th century, their numbers began to increase, though, as tribes struggled to reclaim their lost identities.

Modoc

When they first came into contact with white people, about the beginning of the 19th century, the Modoc lived along the Lost River and around the lakes along the borders of California and Oregon. They shared the area with the Klamath tribe—Klamath to the north, Modoc to the south—and spoke the same dialect of the Penutian language.

Pre-Contact

Before Europeans arrived in the Americas.

The Modoc way of life had more in common with the Plateau peoples to the East than with the Californians. They were also unusual among Californian peoples in resisting white settlement. There were no more than 2,000 Modoc in Pre-Contact times, and by the middle of the 19th century, their numbers had shrunk to a few hundred after a succession of epidemics.

Villages and camps

The Modoc lived in about 25 villages, each with its own headman and shaman (medicine man or woman) but came together as one community in a crisis. Everybody left their villages in spring and moved from camp to camp until fall, exploiting seasonal food supplies. In camp, they lived in shelters made from frames of willow poles stuck into the ground, tied together at the top, and covered with mats woven from tule, a bulrush that grew abundantly in the lakes.

Curriculum Context

Students learning about the diversity of Native American shelters and housing might be asked to describe temporary and permanent Modoc dwellings

Winter homes

In winter, when snow could gather in 6-foot (2-m) drifts, the Modoc people returned to their villages. Here, they lived in lodges, built in round pits 15–40 feet (4.5–12 m) wide and 3–4 feet (1–1.2 m) deep. Stout wooden poles around the edge supported a system of rafters. The Modoc covered the inside of this framework with woven grass mats and the outside with a layer of bark topped with earth from the pit. A hole in the middle of the roof served as a chimney for a fire directly below, a ventilator, a window, and an entrance and exit; the only way in or out of a lodge was by using a ladder. Usually, two or three families shared a lodge.

The sweatlodge

Each Modoc village also had a sweatlodge—a small, airtight structure in which people poured water on heated rocks to produce steam. Men and women used it both for keeping themselves clean and for religious rituals led by the shaman: mostly prayers to spirits of the moon, stars, sky, and animals.

Following the food

Modoc men used nets, traps, hook and line, and spears to catch fish from the lakes and rivers. A seasonal favorite was salmon, caught as they swam upriver to spawn. The men made dugout cedar canoes or rafts of logs tied together with tule for fishing and hunted small game, deer, elk, and antelope.

Modoc

Language:	Penutian
Area:	Basin and Plateau
Reservation:	Oklahoma, but most Modoc today live in Oregon
Population:	2,000 Pre-Contact; approximately 600 today
Housing:	Shelters in summer, lodges in winter
European contact:	Settlers in the 1840s
Neighbors:	Klamath
Lifestyle:	Nomadic hunter-gatherers
Food:	Fish, game, and wild plants
Crafts:	Basketry

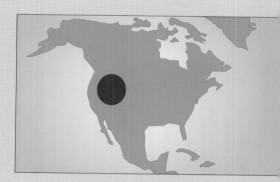

The Modoc lived on the Lost River and lakes of California and Oregon.

Modoc women gathered wild plants and berries and dug roots, such as wild potato. They used tule and other rushes and grasses to weave clothes and mats, and twined them together to create baskets.

In about 1800, the Modoc made indirect contact with white society. By trading with and raiding neighboring tribes, they acquired cloth and metal tools and pots for the first time. They also made contact with some Plains peoples. By the 1830s, they were using horses and had begun wearing skins rather than woven clothing.

The beginning of the end

Late in 1843, a team lead by John Charles Fremont surveyed the Lost River area. As a result, wagon trains began to come through Modoc territory in increasing numbers, following the Applegate Trail down into California. The increased traffic scared away much of the game in the area, and the Modoc began to go hungry. In 1847, an epidemic killed a third of the tribe. Modoc shamans decided the whites were to blame for all the tribe's miseries. The Modoc attacked the next wagon train to arrive, killing several dozen settlers.

Gold rush leads to war

An uneasy truce between the Modoc and the whites followed. Then, in 1851, gold was found nearby. Miners flocked to the area, displacing the Modoc. Skirmishes over land resulted in several deaths, mostly of Modoc who got in the way of a miner's claim. In 1852, a war party killed more than 70 whites at Tule Lake. In retaliation, Ben Wright of Yreka invited 46 Modoc leaders to peace talks and killed 41 of them. The bad feeling between the whites and the Modoc after these incidents came to a head in the Modoc War of 1872–1873, which ended with the tribe defeated and its leaders executed. The survivors were sent to a reservation in Indian Territory; some Modoc remain there today, in what is now Oklahoma.

Applegate Trail

A wilderness trail from the eastern states to the Willamette Valley in Oregon, established in 1846 as a less dangerous route than the Oregon Trail. It branches from the Oregon Trail at Fort Hall, Idaho, and passes through the Nevada desert into northern California.

Curriculum Context

The relationships between mineral prospectors and Native Americans are an important factor when considering the impact of Europeans on indigenous societies.

Mogollon

The Mogollon, or Mountain People, are named after the small, twisting mountain range that runs along the border between southern Arizona and New Mexico, where they established settlements in the high valleys. They were the first prehistoric people of the Southwest to practice agriculture on a regular basis—starting about the third century CE—with crops of corn, beans, tobacco, squash, and cotton.

The Mogollon did not develop the more sophisticated farming techniques of their Anasazi and Hohokam contemporaries, but relied on digging-sticks for preparing the soil and on mountain streams for irrigation. As a result, the Mogollon had to supplement the limited amount of food that they were able to grow by hunting small birds and animals and gathering roots, berries, seeds, nuts, and insects.

Their agricultural efforts did, however, lead to the establishment of permanent villages along ridges above the valleys where they grew their crops. These were easier to defend than valley settlements. Mogollon villages consisted of pit houses made from log frames covered with roofs of saplings, reeds, and mud. Later they also built a few larger buildings to serve as kivas—ceremonial and meeting houses.

After about 1000 CE, the Mogollon came increasingly under the influence of the Anasazi. One consequence of this, and of their growing population, was that the Mogollon abandoned their pit houses in favor of above-ground pueblos made from adobe—bricks of sun-dried clay mixed with straw.

Skilled artisans
Although much of their handicraft was relatively unsophisticated, the Mogollon were skillful weavers.

Curriculum Context

Students learning about the progression to urban living may be asked to analyze the development of Mogollon agriculture and villages.

Fragments of clothing and blankets made from cotton, feathers, and fur yarn have been found by archeologists at Mogollon sites. The Mogollon were excellent basketmakers, too, and also produced a variety of stone, wood, and bone artifacts.

Fabulous pottery

Following the Anasazi example, the Mogollon improved their crude pottery of brown, coiled clay by covering it with a fine slip before firing it. This allowed them to paint it with intricate, geometric designs.

Mimbres pottery

The most dramatic—and best-known—product of Mogollon culture comes from a small group who lived in southwestern New Mexico. These people, known as the Mimbres, produced some of the most exquisite and distinctive pottery of the prehistoric Southwest region. Many Mimbres pots are beautifully painted shallow bowls, with mythical people, animals, and birds depicted in black and white. The designs show a sense of pattern and movement unequaled in any other pottery of the period.

Almost all Mimbres pots recovered from excavations had been ritually "killed" by having a hole broken through the center—this released the pot's spirit into the next world. Most Mimbres pots have been found with burials, so they were probably made specifically as grave offerings.

Sudden departure

The Mogollon's unique culture declined rapidly after 1200 CE and had disappeared completely by 1400. Mysteriously, at some point the last of the Mogollon abruptly abandoned their villages—nobody knows why. Most of the survivors were absorbed into Anasazi communities. Only a few retained their separate, Mogollon identities. It is their blood that flows in the veins of the modern Zuni.

Naskapi

The Algonquian-speaking Naskapi live in the Subarctic areas of Labrador and Quebec, to the east of Hudson Bay and James Bay. However, in the past their influence extended as far south as the St. Lawrence River through their close relatives, the Montagnais.

Subarctic winters are intensely cold with little sunlight. Summers are short, with swarms of mosquitoes and black fly in the swampy areas. Few peoples share the Naskapi experience of surviving in such a harsh environment with scarce and unreliable resources. So the Naskapi had little contact with outside groups.

Naskapi lifestyle

The area is too far north for farming, and with rivers frozen for much of the year the Naskapi rely primarily on caribou hunting for meat and clothing. They also hunt moose, waterfowl, and small game animals, such as hare, porcupine, and beaver. During the summer, the Naskapi fish mainly for salmon, eels, and trout.

Climate also affects the social organization of the Naskapi. Scarce, unpredictable resources prevented the formation of large settlements with one leader. Instead, tribes are composed of numerous small family bands, often little more than an extended family group.

These bands meet only on rare occasions during the summer, when resources are plentiful and travel is easier. Summer meetings are times of rejoicing and feasting, when relationships between kinfolk are reaffirmed and marriages are arranged. The bands fish together and assemble for group hunts.

The fact that there was no political unit meant that Naskapi chiefs had little say, and authority rested primarily with individual family heads. This resulted in a genuine democracy.

Curriculum Context

Naskapi society is a good example of Native American life and social organization shaped by the climate.

European influence

From the 16th century onward, exposure to outside influences resulted in the Naskapi acquiring many European goods, including guns, steel tools, kettles, traps, and cloth. The southern groups, with access to the St. Lawrence River, also became heavily involved in the French fur trade, which remained important to the Naskapi into the 19th century.

However, European influence did not undermine traditional aspects of Naskapi life. Authority remained with the family heads, and the tribe continued to use birchbark canoes and birchbark-covered wigwams. Hunting remained their main means of survival.

Wigwam

The Eastern name for a domed dwelling consisting of a single room, formed on a frame of arched poles and covered with a roofing material such as birchbark, grass, or hides.

Beliefs and rituals

The Naskapi still maintain ancient beliefs today. Their god Chilkapes is regarded not only as a destroyer of monsters but also as a trickster who deceives people. The Naskapi also believe in a figure called Mistapeo, leader of a tribe of nature spirits, with whom only shamans can communicate. The dangers of life in the harsh Subarctic have given rise to belief in a host of malevolent ogres and dwarfs, who are said to lure the unwary to untimely deaths.

The Naskapi honor and revere animals. Every hunter pays homage to his prey by preserving and decorating a part of each animal and addressing its carcass in respectful terms. Elaborate rituals are carried out before a hunting expedition to assess the prospects of success and a safe return for the hunter. Before a caribou hunt the bones of a caribou are burned and then examined for signs that might indicate successful hunting to come. Naskapi hunters wear distinctive tailored caribou skin coats during the summer hunting season. These coats are painted with red markings—parallel lines, triangles and leaf shapes—which represent the caribou's antlers and tracks.

Navajo

The Navajo of the Southwest live on a reservation that covers 25,000 square miles (64,750 sq. km) in Arizona, with other settlements in New Mexico and Utah. It is the largest reservation in the United States.

The name *Navajo*, or *Navaho*, means "great fields." It was first used by the Spanish, who encountered small nomadic bands living near an abandoned pueblo called Navahu. Since the Pueblo people called the nomads *Apachu*, or "enemy," the Spanish named them *L'Apache de Navahu*. The Navajo call themselves *Dine*, or *Dene*, which simply means "the people."

The Navajo early lifestyle

The Athapascan language of the Navajo is related to dialects spoken by Native Americans in northwestern Canada. It is believed that the Navajo migrated from the far north to the Southwest between 1000 and 1400 CE. They are close relatives of the Apache and at first lived a nomadic life as hunter–gatherers.

The men hunted deer, antelope, and rabbit, and the women collected piñon nuts, cactus, yucca fruit, and berries. Navajo warriors also made frequent raids on the Pueblo fields and villages to get agricultural produce such as corn, beans, and squash.

New skills and crafts

In the mid-16th century, the Spanish moved into the Southwest from Mexico, providing the Navajo with new peoples to raid. Throughout the 1600s and 1700s they continued to attack the Pueblo, from whom they also learned about agriculture and weaving. From the Spanish, the Navajo acquired horses and sheep.

Despite beginning to plant crops and tend sheep, the Navajo did not settle down. Horses taken from the

Spanish enabled them to extend their raiding over larger areas. In 1821, the Navajo continued to raid Mexican villages in the Southwest. The Navajo also attacked Americans, after the United States gained control of the Southwest in 1848.

The Navajo had some justification for feeling aggressive. When the war between the United States and Mexico started in 1846, the U.S. government promised the citizens of the Southwest that they would be protected by the army. The Navajo were not regarded as citizens, and raids against their homes by Mexicans and Americans went unpunished.

War with the United States

The Navajo were persuaded to sign a treaty with the United States in 1848, and relationships were peaceful until the 1850s, when U.S. troops shot Navajo horses on pasture land near Fort Defiance. The area had been Navajo grazing land for generations, and the tribe retaliated by raiding army horse herds to replace their stock. The army attacked the Navajo, and a war followed in which the Navajo were commanded by two chiefs, Manuelito and Barboncito.

A truce was made in 1861, but white settlers were eager to acquire Navajo lands. In 1863, Colonel Christopher "Kit" Carson was sent to solve the "Navajo problem." He knew it was useless to send troops into the canyons, where many Navajo were in hiding. Instead, he had the Navajo fields and orchards destroyed, and their horses and sheep shot. The Navajo were forced to surrender or starve.

Reservation life

After their defeat, the Navajo were forced to march 300 miles (480 km) west to Bosque Redondo, a barren area in the Pecos River Valley. The journey became known as the "Long Walk." Many died during the journey, and conditions at Bosque Redondo were terrible. The land was infertile, there was little water and no firewood, and hardly any food. Great numbers of Navajo died from disease and starvation.

Finally, in 1868, Manuelito and Barboncito were allowed to visit Washington to explain the Navajo's desperate plight. The Navajo were granted a tiny reservation in their former homeland on lands the Americans did not want. Each family was given two sheep, and the Navajo returned to rebuild their lives.

More land was added in 1875 and 1884. In the early 20th century, it was discovered that the land that had been returned was rich in coal, oil, and uranium. In the 1920s, the Navajo set up the Navajo General Council (later the Navajo Nation Council) to negotiate mining rights with the U.S. government. Tribal income was used to purchase more land and livestock. The Navajo

Navajo

Language:	Athapascan
Area:	Southwest
Reservation:	Arizona, New Mexico, and Utah
Population:	20,000 in 1900; over 220,000 today
Housing:	Hogans
European contact:	Spanish settlers from Mexico in the 1600s
Neighbors:	Pueblo, Apache, and Hopi
Lifestyle:	Originally hunter-gatherers; later farmers, ranchers, and traders
Food:	Wild plants, game, and some farming
Crafts:	Weaving, silverwork, and jewelry making

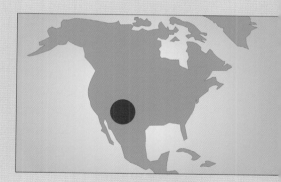

The Navajo reservation is the largest in the United States.

Navajo women and children sit outside their adobe hut in this photo that dates from around 1914, before the Navajo benefited from the minerals found on their land.

settled and began to prosper. Today, there are about 220,000 Navajo. Tribal income is big business and is run by professional managers.

Finding their place

Navajo family life continues in much the same way that it always has, although the people have bitter memories of life at Bosque Redondo and their former treatment by the Spanish, Mexicans, and Americans. This has caused many Navajo to follow their traditional beliefs and customs rather than accept the values of the wider United States.

However, despite their resentment toward the United States, more than 3,000 Navajo served the country during World War II. Navajo Code Talkers, as they were known, transmitted important U.S. military messages in their native language, and the system was so successful that the Japanese were never able to crack the code.

Traditional housing

Many Navajo families still use the traditional hogan, a conical or octagonal building made from a wooden framework. This framework is cemented with mud or

Curriculum Context

The Navajo hogan is an example of how Native American housing can be linked to religion.

adobe (sun-dried earth and straw). The hogan is both a dwelling and a sacred place, with its door facing east to catch the first rays of the rising sun. The Navajo regard the sun with great reverence and call it the Life-Bringer.

Hogans are built in scattered, isolated parts of the vast reservation. To visit one's neighbor might mean a journey on horseback of several hours, and this reflects the Navajo's former seminomadic life.

Ritual and ceremony

Ceremony is thought of as a symbolic journey through the stages of a person's life. A child's first laugh is marked by an important feast, as is the occasion when the child receives a name. For Navajo girls, the coming of age is celebrated by a major ritual that lasts four days. Everything of importance to the Navajo individual is marked by ceremony and ritual.

Sings

The navajo hold ceremonies, called sings, to heal the sick or bring blessings. These ceremonies often take place in the hogan. Some may last as long as nine days and require the ceremony leader, or singer, to remember several complicated series of songs. The Navajo believe that any mistake in the songs will bring bad luck. Sand paintings form part of these ceremonies.

These paintings are made by the singer using sand, pollen, and colored powders made from crushed rock. The sand is sifted through the fingers to form complex designs depicting the Yeis, or Holy People, and to show major events from the legends that record the people's history. After each ceremony, the painting is destroyed.

Navajo crafts

Visitors to the Southwest are more familiar with Navajo weaving and silverwork. Both use symbols based on the land in which the Navajo live. Brilliantly colored geometric patterns on Navajo blankets suggest the rugged canyons of the area and the play of light and shadow on them.

Nez Percé

The Nez Percé lived in the Plateau region of the Northwest, an area of mountain passes, high grassy valleys, and meadows through which the Snake River runs. The area is rich in game, fish, roots, and berries, all of which the Nez Percé used. They traded with neighboring tribes, and when white explorers and settlers came to the region, the Nez Percé lived in peace with them.

Curriculum Context

It is interesting to compare Nez Percé political systems and civic values with those of Europeans in North America.

Nez Percé means "pierced noses" in French, but although some of the tribes living nearby may have worn nose rings, there is no evidence the Nez Percé did so. They lived in several small groups with no overall tribal leadership and referred to themselves by local names such as *Numiipu* or *Chutepalu*.

Lifestyle and culture

The Nez Percé originally occupied a huge area in southeast Washington State, northeast Oregon, and central Idaho. They lived by streams and rivers in bands made up of extended families. They wore deerskin clothes and ate venison, salmon, roots, and berries.

In summer, the bands traveled widely on foot or by dugout canoe in search of fish, game, roots, and berries. Much of the food that they hunted and gathered they dried and stored for winter. In winter, they stayed by the rivers in large multifamily houses made of a timber framework covered with woven mats. There were several family fires along the center of each house floor and much sharing of food.

In fall, when families returned from their wanderings and gathered again at the winter settlements, there were many celebrations and festivals. One of these, the Keuuyit, was to thank the animals, fish, and plants that had provided food for them. The Nez Percé also regularly honored a guardian spirit in dances and ceremonies, since the guardian spirit was thought to be responsible for everything that affected their lives.

After horses were introduced to the region in the early 1700s, the bands went farther afield and hunted buffalo on the Plains. They became famous for breeding horses, especially spotted Appaloosas. They used folding hide pouches—called *parfleches*—and bags of woven hemp to carry meat and clothes. The woven bags and the bows, made from sheep horn, were much sought after by other local peoples. The Nez Percé traded them at fairs, along with buffalo skins and robes, and sometimes horses. They grew rich through horse-breeding and trading, and, by the 1880s, some wealthy Nez Percé families owned as many as 1,500 horses.

Curriculum Context

Horse breeding and trading was the most important economic activity in Nez Percé life.

There were about 7,000 Nez Percé in 1805, when they encountered an expedition of white explorers from the United States led by Lewis and Clark. The Nez Percé helped the explorers and remained friendly to the white settlers, traders, and Christian missionaries who arrived later.

Two different bands

The Nez Percé were in fact made up of two different bands—the Upper and Lower Nez Percé—who occupied separate lands but shared hunting grounds. A split began to develop between the two groups as they adjusted to the changes introduced by settlers. The Upper Nez Percé converted to Christianity and began to give up their traditional way of life. The Lower Nez Percé, who lived in the Wallowa and Grande Ronde Valleys, rejected Christianity, remaining independent.

In 1855, the U.S. authorities proposed a treaty with the Nez Percé. Under this agreement, the Nez Percé were to sell their lands and move onto the 7.5-million-acre (3-million-ha) Lapwai Reservation. The Upper Nez

Curriculum Context

At different times, the Nez Percé both cooperated with and rejected the European settlers.

Percé, led by a chief called Lawyer, signed the treaty, but the Lower Nez Percé, led by Chief Joseph, did not. Chief Joseph's father, Tuekakas, had warned his son never to sell his people's lands to the whites.

Conflict with the United States

In the 1860s, gold was found in the Wallowa Mountains. The American authorities wanted to reduce the size of Nez Percé territory to release the lands for mining. Lawyer signed away the Lower Nez Percé lands, but Chief Joseph refused to comply, pointing out that his people had never signed the earlier treaty.

Tensions increased over the next 10 years. In 1877, the Lower Nez Percé were given just 30 days to move to

Nez Percé

Language:	Sahaptian
Area:	Northwest; original lands covered southeast Washington, northeast Oregon, and central Idaho
Reservation:	Lapwai, Idaho
Population:	About 7,000 in 1805; approximately 4,000 today
Housing:	Wooden mat-covered houses and hide tepees
European contact:	Lewis and Clark expedition, 1805; some earlier contact with French explorers and European traders
Neighbors:	Walla Walla, Cayuse, Coeur d'Alene, Flathead, Shoshoni, and Bannock
Lifestyle:	Originally hunter-gatherers; later buffalo hunters, horse breeders, and traders
Food:	Large game, salmon, roots, and berries
Crafts:	Woven bags and horn bows

In the early 1800s, the Nez Percé were friendly with the white settlers in their territory. By the end of the century, the white settlers had driven the tribe from their homeland and killed many people.

the Lapwai reservation. Joseph and his followers began to move, but the Nez Percé were angry and indignant. A band of young warriors killed 11 white settlers. In retaliation, the U.S. Army attacked the Nez Percé. Chief Joseph now took command of his people against the U.S. forces. This resulted in the Nez Percé War. However, the conflict ended with Joseph's surrender. After the surrender, a few Nez Percé escaped to Canada. Some were sent to the Lapwai reservation, but most were taken to the Indian Territory in the Midwest. Chief Joseph continued to ask the authorities to allow his people to return to the Northwest.

CHIEF JOSEPH.
NEZ PERCES.

The situation today

In 1863, the size of the Nez Percé reservation had been reduced to one tenth of its original size. In 1893, it was reduced again to a tenth of this. Despite disease and the loss of their land, the Nez Percé held on to their language and culture. In 1950, they numbered 1,400, and today there are over 4,000 of them. From their headquarters in northwest Idaho, the Nez Percé Tribal Council administers social services for its people and strives for economic growth. Now it hopes to regain at least part of its lost territories.

Although most Nez Percé were taken to the Indian Territory in the Midwest after the war, Chief Joseph was sent to Colville Reservation in Washington State, where he remained for the rest of his life, dying there in 1904.

Nootka

The Nootka are a Northwest Coast people. They traditionally occupied villages along the western coast of Vancouver Island and Cape Flattery on the northeastern tip of Washington State. They speak Nootka, part of the Wakashan language family. Today, the people are often known by their traditional native name, *Nuu-Chah-Nulth*.

Skilled whale hunters

The Nootka were the only Northwest group who hunted whales. Those among them who did the hunting were highly skilled. For this reason, the whaler was regarded as a household leader or chief.

The secrets and rituals of whaling were inherited by the son of the household leader. Before the hunt, the whaler would take part in an elaborate ritual, which he hoped would result in a safe and successful hunt. During the ritual, the whaler would chant secret songs and mimic the whale's movements.

Large dugout canoes were used for whaling. Having sighted a whale, the whaler would drive his kill toward the land so that he could tow the carcass to shore more easily. Harpoons on the end of long lines with sealskin floats were used in the hunt. Successful hunts were always celebrated with a feast.

Nootka lifestyle

Salmon was an important source of food. In the warm months, the Nootka moved from one fishing ground to another, following the fish. As winter neared, they returned to their more permanent settlements. The Nootka built large rectangular longhouses of cedar planks, which were typical of Northwest culture. Each housed a number of families. Carved and painted cedar totem poles were placed at the front of the houses.

Curriculum Context

Nootka culture and values can be compared with those of their Northwest Coast neighbors.

Longhouse

A communal house shared by several families. Longhouses measured up to 200 feet (60 m) in length and were built of post frames covered in planks.

Canoes, also built of cedar, were used for traveling, fishing, and for hunting whales.

The Nootka made their clothing from bark and animal skins or traded their blankets with the Tlingit for dog hair or mountain sheep wool. They often painted their faces and bodies in bright colors, applying the paint over a layer of bear grease.

Customs and ceremonies

The Nootka enjoyed games and competitions. One of these was the laughing competition, in which two teams sat opposite one another. Onlookers placed bets on which team could maintain serious faces the longest. The losing team would be the one on which an individual broke into a smile.

The major celebration of the year was the Wolf Dance, or Nutlam, in which a symbolic kidnapping of children

Nootka

Language:	Wakashan
Area:	Northwest Coast
Reservation:	Vancouver Island, British Columbia
Population:	Pre-Contact 15,000; approximately 6,700 today
Housing:	Rectangular plank houses
European contact:	British explorers under James Cook, 1778
Neighbors:	Salish, Kwakiutl
Lifestyle:	Whale hunters and fishermen
Food:	Whale and salmon, shellfish, small game, and fruit
Crafts:	Carvings, including totem poles and masks

The Nootka were the only Northwest Coast group to hunt whales.

by wolf spirits took place, and young men were initiated into the tribe. Feasting was an important part of this social occasion.

Nootka today

Today, there are 1,600 Nootka living on reserve lands in southern British Columbia, out of a total population of over 6,700. The main occupations of the modern Nootka are fishing and working in the canning industry. In the past, the Nootka also worked in the logging industry.

In 1973, the Nootka formed a society called the West Coast District Society of Indian Chiefs, which later became the Nuu-Chah-Nulth Tribal Council. Together with other Native American peoples, the Nootka have entered into new treaty discussions with the governments of British Columbia and Canada. They are negotiating over a number of issues, including land, fishing, and logging rights.

Around 1910, a Nootka man takes a ceremonial bath before a whale hunt, one of the elaborate rituals associated with whaling.

Olmec

The Olmec were a sophisticated people who lived in southern Mexico in ancient times. Their civilization flourished for over eight centuries, from about 1200 BCE to about 400 BCE. The Olmec made great advances in art, religion, and technology, influencing later civilizations such as the Maya, Toltec, and Aztecs.

The Olmec people lived in the hot, swampy lowlands around the Bay of Campeche in the Gulf of Mexico. The word *Olmec*, meaning "people from the land of rubber," was first used in the 1920s, when archaeologists began to study the culture. The main Olmec sites that have been excavated are at San Lorenzo, La Venta, and Tres Zapotes. These three cities flourished at different points in Olmec history, but they had in common the production of giant carved stone heads.

Lifestyle of the Olmec

The Olmec were farmers, traders, fishermen, builders, and artists. They dug ditches to carry water from the rivers to their fields, where they grew corn, beans, and other crops. They also ate fish, game, and wild dogs.

In Olmec cities, houses and temples were built on earth mounds and platforms, raising them above the low ground that was prone to flood after heavy rain. The timber and thatch houses were laid out on a grid pattern that ran from north to south. These houses were built around walled plazas.

Olmec cities included ball courts, where ceremonial ball games were played. Imposing pyramid temples were built on the highest ground in the city centers.

The Olmec were a highly organized people with a rigid social structure in which the kings and priests ruled over the citizens. Recently discovered carvings suggest

Curriculum Context

The development of Olmec civilization can only be understood by interpreting archaeological evidence.

that rulers and warriors wore elaborate headdresses and chest armor and that, in general, the people wore few clothes and adorned themselves with headbands, jewelry, and tattoos.

Olmec culture

The Olmec were skilled astrologers who developed a calendar based on the movements of the sun and moon. The recent discovery of a huge stone slab inscribed with over 450 hieroglyphs shows that they also had their own form of writing.

Olmec religion was based on the worship of a fierce jaguar god—half man, half beast—who was probably the guardian of the underworld. To honor this god, Olmec priests, or shamans, wore jaguar masks at ceremonies. Other deities included fire and corn gods, and the feathered serpent god who became popular later with other peoples in Mesoamerica.

Hieroglyph
A character used in a system of pictorial writing.

Olmec

Language:	Unknown
Area:	South-central Mexico, around Veracruz and Tabasco
Reservation:	None
Population:	Unknown
Housing:	Timber and thatch houses; pyramid temples built on earth mounds
European contact:	None
Neighbors:	Unknown
Lifestyle:	Farming, fishing, trading, and crafts
Food:	Corn, beans, fish, deer, and wild dogs
Crafts:	Sculpting giant stone heads and smaller carvings; jewelry making and mosaics

The ancient Olmec culture influenced the later great civilizations of southern Mexico, including the Maya, Toltec, and Aztecs.

Giant sculptures

The first of the stone-carved heads for which the Olmec are best known was discovered in 1862. Since then, 15 more heads have been unearthed. Some stand 5–10 feet (1.5–3 m) high and weigh over 20 tons (18 t). They are made of basalt (volcanic rock). With no metal tools, the sculptors carved the stone by scouring the surface with natural abrasives such as sand. The stones came from the highlands up to 50 miles (75 km) away. They were rolled on logs or sledges to rivers, then ferried downstream on giant rafts.

One of the stone heads at La Venta. Many archaeologists believe that the sculptures represent kings, warriors, or ball players. The faces of the sculptures all have wide, flat noses and full lips and appear to be realistic portraits.

The Olmec also made smaller statues of gods in stone, clay, and wood. They carved giant stone slabs and pillars, and cut rock walls and thrones. Their craftspeople also made jewelry, weapons, tools, and large mosaics. Olmec traders traveled widely to obtain jade and other semiprecious stones for carving.

End of the civilization

About 400 BCE, the Olmec civilization suddenly ended for reasons that are not fully understood. Sculptures in major settlements were smashed. One theory is that the people overthrew the leaders. Another possibility is that the Olmec were defeated in war.

Curriculum Context

Sculpture, monument building, glyphic writing, and the calendar are major Olmec contributions to civilization in Mesoamerica.

Paiute

From prehistoric times, the Paiute inhabited a huge area of the vast, rocky Great Basin, from what is now Oregon in the north to Death Valley in the southwest and Utah in the east. There was not enough food in any single place in these dry lands to feed the people for long. They traveled constantly in order to take advantage of seasonal supplies of fruit and game.

Wickiup
The Southwestern or Western name for a domed dwelling consisting of a single room, formed on a frame of arched poles and covered with a roofing material such as birchbark, grass, or hides.

During the summer, the Paiute lived in cone-shaped shelters—called wickiups—made of branches covered with brush or reeds. In winter, they built stronger structures, sometimes underground, to provide shelter from freezing temperatures, snow, and violent storms.

Hunting and gathering
The main foods of the Paiute were plants and small game, especially jackrabbits. These provided meat for food and fur and skins for clothes and shelter.

Women gathered wild fruit and seeds, and dug for roots and bulbs with digging sticks. Piñon nuts were a major source of food. In fall, women used poles to knock the cones from the trees. These were roasted in pits to separate the seeds or stored for the winter.

Local differences
The Paiute in the north and south of the region led fairly different lives and developed separate cultures. Northern Paiute hunted deer and marmots in the hills, netted and speared fish from willow platforms on the rivers, and made duck decoys from reeds to lure wildfowl close enough to kill. Southern Paiute hunted lizards, snakes, insects, and small game. Southwestern Paiute grew corn, squash, sunflowers, and beans.

The northern Paiute called themselves *Nuwu*, which means "the people." They lived in extended family units but came together in large groups for the May fishing season, the piñon nut harvest in the fall, and the November rabbit hunt, when the jackrabbits were driven into nets and killed. To strengthen their ties of kinship, Paiute performed tribal ceremonies in which men and women danced in a circle around a central pole or around a singer.

The Paiute believed there were spirits in every part of nature and showed respect to these spirits by praying to them, especially for rain or for a successful hunt.

The southern Paiute were basketweavers. Their finely woven baskets were used to store food, and larger baskets were used for carrying. Food was cooked in baskets using water heated with hot stones. Paiute weaving skills were famed throughout the region, and baskets were traded with the Hopi, Zuni, and Navajo.

Paiute

Language:	Uto-Aztecan
Area:	Great Basin
Reservation:	Small reservations in Nevada including Pyramid Lake and the Reno-Sparks Colony
Population:	Pre-Contact 15,000; approximately 11,000 today
Housing:	Tepee or wickiup
European contact:	Spanish settlers in the 1700s
Neighbors:	Shoshoni, Bannock, Ute, Gosiute, and Navajo
Lifestyle:	Nomadic hunter-gatherers
Food:	Small game, wild plants
Crafts:	Basket weaving and beadwork

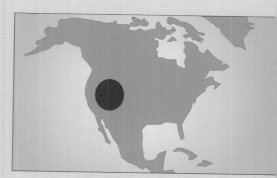

The Paiute showed great ingenuity in surviving for centuries in the harsh landscape of the Great Basin.

Curriculum Context

Students learning about the attitudes and policies toward Native Americans by various groups of Europeans can usefully study the history of the Paiute from the late 1700s.

European contact

In the late 1700s, Spanish missionaries in Utah began to baptize and enslave the Paiute. In the 1850s, the Mormons arrived and freed the Paiute from the Spanish but took the best lands for themselves. Around the same time, gold was discovered in California and Nevada, and silver deposits were found in the Reno–Carson City area. Prospectors and settlers arrived in large numbers.

In the 1860s, the Paiute were moved onto reservations, where many died from diseases and epidemics. Life on the reservations destroyed the Paiute's traditional, nomadic way of life and weakened their culture. By the 1870s, most Paiute had become dependent on the government or worked for the whites for wages.

In 1965, the Indian Claims Commission awarded the southern Paiute $8.25 million in compensation for lost lands. Today, the Paiute live on reservations scattered throughout Nevada. In Utah and California, they share reservations with groups such as the Shoshoni.

Wovoka and the Ghost Dance

In the late 1880s, a Paiute shaman (medicine man) called Wovoka founded the Ghost Dance religion—a faith that mixed Native American beliefs and Christian ideas. On New Year's Day 1889, Wovoka had a vision in which God told him that if Native Americans lived peaceful and industrious lives, a messiah (savior) would come to unite them. The whites would be swept away, the buffalo would return, and the traditional ways would be restored. The new religion centered on the Ghost Dance, in which dancers called up the spirits of the dead.

In the late 1880s, the movement spread among the peoples of the Great Basin and the Plains who had lost their lands, including the Lakota Sioux. The U.S. authorities saw the Ghost Dance as a threat, since it was uniting diverse Native American groups. In 1890, at Wounded Knee in South Dakota the U.S. Army massacred hundreds of Lakota Ghost Dance followers, including women and children. By the 1890s, the movement was all but destroyed.

Papago and Pima

The Papago and Pima live in the dusty, desert country of southern Arizona and northern Mexico. They have lived near each other for hundreds of years and have inherited Hohokam culture and technology. Today they share a similar culture and lifestyle.

Lifestyle of the O'odham

The Pima call themselves the *Akimel O'odham*—the "river people." They settled the Snake and Gila river valleys, growing corn, squash, beans, wheat, and cotton.

The Papago call themselves the *Tohono O'odham*—the "desert people." They moved between their summer and winter villages to take advantage of seasonal rains. In winter, they lived in upland villages fed by mountain springs. In summer, they moved to lowland villages to farm fields watered by annual floods.

As well as raising crops, the Papago and Pima hunted rabbits, rodents, deer, and mountain sheep and gathered wild foods such as grass seeds and mesquite beans. The women harvested the fruit of the saguaro cactus with long poles. It was eaten fresh or dried, and the juice was extracted to make syrup, jam, and wine.

Housing and crafts

Desert plants provided materials for tools, clothes, and shelter. The Papago and Pima lived in domed houses covered with bark, thatch, or animal hides and wove rushes and willow into fine bowls and baskets. The devil's claw plant provided darker strands to weave pictures and patterns, which often depicted themes from traditional legends.

Ceremonies and beliefs

The most important ceremonies were linked with bringing rain. The Viikita ceremony was held in June or July, before the rainy season. The Papago and Pima drank wine made from fermented saguaro juice during the ceremony to please the rain spirits.

Their most important gods were called Earthmaker and Elder Brother. The Papago and Pima believed that Elder Brother helped Earthmaker shape the world and lead the people from the underworld. Myths also featured fearsome monsters that ate human flesh.

European contact

In the 1690s, Spanish colonists introduced horses, cattle, and wheat, but they also forced the Papago and Pima to work for them and demanded yearly tribute. They built garrisons and missions, and converted many native people to Christianity. From a combination of Catholicism and traditional tribal beliefs grew Sonoran Catholicism, a religion that is still popular in the Southwest today.

Papago and Pima

Language:	Uto-Aztecan
Area:	Southwest
Reservation:	Several in southern Arizona
Population:	Papago: about 50,000 Pre-Contact; approximately 20,000 today.
	Pima: about 50,000 Pre-Contact; approximately 14,000 today
Housing:	Domed thatch, hide, or bark houses
European contact:	Spaniards in the 1690s
Neighbors:	Hopi, Navaho, and Apache
Lifestyle:	Hunter-gatherers and farmers
Food:	Wild plants, small game, corn, squash, and other crops
Crafts:	Basket weaving

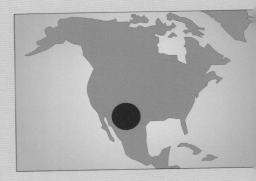

The Papago and Pima have grown crops in the dry desert country of the Southwest for hundreds of years.

Under the terms of the Gadsden Purchase of 1853, the lands of the Papago and Pima were split: the northern half became part of the United States, the southern part was in Mexico.

The Papago and Pima helped the U.S. Army against the Apache, their traditional enemies, and fought for the Union in the Civil War of the 1860s, defeating the Confederates under the Pima leader Antonio Azul.

Land loss and reservations

In the late 1800s, settlers encroached on tribal lands and confined the Papago and Pima to reservations. Their seminomadic way of life was destroyed, and adults had no choice but to work for wages. Children were sent away to be "civilized." South of the border, Mexican ranchers and miners also took Papago lands. The Pima, too, were settled on small reservations that had once been part of their homelands. Upstream, ranchers and miners diverted rivers, and soon the Pima lands were dry. The Pima call the period from the 1870s to the early 1900s the Forty Years of Famine. During this time, Presbyterian missionaries visited the reservations and converted many Pima to Christianity.

In 1911, in response to the U.S. government's allocation of only 10 acres (4 ha) of irrigable land for every Pima, the people set up a business committee. In 1916 and again in 1937, Papago reservation lands were enlarged. Today the Tohono O'odham reservation is one of the largest in the United States. From the 1930s, O'odham on government work projects developed their lands, sinking wells and building roads and schools. In 1936 and 1937, tribal governments and constitutions were established.

Today, there are around 20,000 Papago and 14,000 Pima. Many live and work on reservation lands. Others work in Tucson, Phoenix, and nearby cities.

Gadsden Purchase

A region in southern Arizona and New Mexico, purchased by the United States from Mexico in 1853 to allow for the construction of a southern transcontinental railroad.

Curriculum Context

The Papago and Pima experienced many of the typical problems faced by Native Americans after Europeans arrived on their lands.

Pomo

For thousands of years, the Pomo lived in the hills and valleys of northern California, from Clear Lake in the east to the Pacific coast in the west. They included more than 70 different groups, each with its own language or dialect. They lived in villages of wickiups (simple thatched huts) that were built around a central meeting house or dance hall.

Acorns were a staple food—pounded into flour to make meal or bread. The people also gathered roots and berries, hunted game, and fished in Clear Lake from reed boats. In summer, local groups came together for a ceremony called Big Time, which lasted for several days and included feasting and dancing.

The Pomo were skilled craftspeople, known for their beadwork and basket weaving. Both men and women wove hats, pots, and baskets using different plant materials. Baskets were decorated with beads or feathers.

European contact

Spanish explorers and Russians came to California, but neither group had much effect on the Pomo. This situation changed in 1848, however, when gold was discovered in California, and the Gold Rush began. Prospectors began flooding into the area. In the rush for riches, the Pomo were driven from their lands. Some were kidnapped and enslaved; others died of diseases brought by the white settlers. In 1856, a Pomo reservation was set up on the coast. In 1868, the U.S. government abolished the reservation, leaving the Pomo homeless, landless, and without legal rights. Many Pomo returned to Clear Lake.

Despite a history of persecution, the Pomo have held onto their culture and traditions. In recent years, their skill as artists and craftspeople has been recognized.

Curriculum Context

Studies of the relationships between Native Americans and various European groups may include an analysis of the role played by prospectors.

Pueblo

The Pueblo of the Southwest were given their name by Spanish settlers because of their settled village lifestyle: in Spanish *pueblo* means "village." Today, there are about 30 Pueblo tribal groups divided into two distinct cultural areas.

The Eastern Pueblo (including Taos and Isleta) are based around the Rio Grande River in central and northern New Mexico, while the Western Pueblo incorporate the Zuni, Acoma, and Laguna in western New Mexico and the Hopi in northeastern Arizona. Including both these areas, the Pueblo speak six distinct languages.

Curriculum Context

Students learning about the Pueblo peoples might be asked to study their diverse languages and tribal groupings.

Pueblo history

Many Pueblo peoples are descendants of the prehistoric Anasazi, who were farmers and skillful potters. The Pueblo period began in about 1300 CE, following the decline of the Anasazi "golden age," which was the result of prolonged droughts, overcrowding, and invading bands of Navajo and Apache. Most of today's Pueblo villages were founded after this period on top of high mesas (steep-sided plateaus) or on flat lands close to water. Acoma village, home to the Acoma, has been inhabited for over 1,000 years, making it the oldest town in the United States.

Spanish colonists

In 1539, the Spanish met the Zuni Pueblo for the first time. A year later, the Spanish explorer Francisco Vasquez de Coronado led another expedition into the Pueblo region to search for Cibola, a legendary land with seven cities of gold and jewels. He retreated after failing to find any treasure.

In 1598, the Spanish occupied Pueblo territory, establishing missions in almost every village. The native people tried to stay friendly with the Spanish

Curriculum Context

The Pueblo revolt is a unique example of successful native resistance to European enroachment. Students might examine its consequences for the development of the Southwest.

and agreed to adopt some European-style systems of government and religious practice. But after being forced to provide slave labor for Spanish ranches and to abandon their own religious practices, a large-scale Pueblo revolt broke out in 1680. They drove the Spanish from the territory, a feat never repeated by another Native American group.

When the Pueblo were reconquered by the Spanish in 1692, they continued to perform their religious kachina ceremonies secretly in their underground ceremonial chambers called kivas.

The two Pueblo groups reacted very differently to Spanish rule. The Eastern Pueblo became practicing Roman Catholics, integrating Christianity into their native religion. The Western Pueblo resisted Spanish influence and kept their own rituals and religion.

Pueblo

Language:	Hopi, Zuni, Keres, Tewa, Tiwa, and Towa
Area:	Southwest
Reservation:	Arizona and New Mexico
Population:	70,000 Pre-Contact; about 53,000 today
Housing:	Multistory stone or mudbrick houses
European contact:	Spanish in 1539
Neighbors:	Navajo and Apache
Lifestyle:	Farmers
Food:	Corn, beans, chilies, squash, melons, mutton, deer, and rabbit
Crafts:	Pottery, basketwork, and weaving

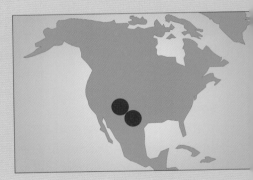

The Eastern and Western Pueblo are two distinct groups in the Southwest.

Reservations

By the end of the 19th century, the Pueblo lands had been reduced in size and made into official reservations. But even there they were not secure. In one case, the U.S. government attempted to take over the mountains and Blue Lake near Taos. In 1928, the Taos Pueblo began a 40-year struggle to recover their sacred land, and their representatives made many trips to Washington DC to plead their case in court. They finally won in 1968.

Recently, low incomes, unemployment, and clashes with the white culture, particularly over exploitation of land, have led to rising tensions on the reservations. However, many Pueblo who leave their villages return on a regular basis to maintain contact with their community and its values.

Pueblo economy

The Pueblo economy was based around agriculture. Now it is supplemented by livestock introduced by the Spanish and by the sale of handicrafts. Crops grown include corn, beans, chilies, melons, squash, and cotton. Men work the fields, weave, build houses, and conduct religious ceremonies. Women prepare the food, care for children, and make baskets and pottery.

Pueblo pottery is still made in the traditional way by coiling clay. Each village has its own unique patterns and styles. Designs are applied using the chewed tip of a yucca leaf as a paintbrush.

Social life

Each Pueblo group acts as a tribe, making its own decisions. There are laws for all aspects of life. Pueblo villages are made up of several extended families, or clans, each with its own secret society and religious duties. Without a central authority, the Pueblo look to these institutions to bind them together.

Curriculum Context

Students can compare the Pueblo political system with that of their Spanish rulers.

Each Pueblo group is led by a council of between 10 and 30 members, including the kiva priests, a war chief, and a ceremonial officer. Under Spanish rule, a governor was added whose responsibilities included acting as a spokesman for the village.

The Taos pueblo has adobe walls several feet thick to protect it from attack. Until the 20th century, it had no doors. To reach the lower floor, inhabitants had to climb up ladders to the roof then come down an inside ladder. If the pueblo was attacked, the outer ladders could be pulled up onto the roof.

Houses

Pueblo villages are honeycombs of two- or three-storied houses made of mudbrick or stone. People enter them by ladders that lead to a hole in the roof. Traditionally, there were no doors, and windows were very small as protection against the variable climate.

Clans and marriage

Clan members have equal status regardless of blood ties. They work together during the harvest and to build new houses. Marriage is always outside the clan. Among the Western Pueblo, family life centers on the mother's line of descent, and women own the fields and houses. Although husbands live with their wife's clan, they often return to their own clan to fulfill religious obligations. As a result, husbands do not play as important a role in bringing up children as do the mother's brother and parents.

Rooms were added as required, so sometimes a whole village could end up living in a single complex building. Modern Pueblo buildings tend to be single-storied, with glass windows and wooden doors.

Religion

Farming is often difficult in this harsh landscape, so the Pueblo have developed an annual round of ceremonies they believe will bring rain and good harvests.

Kachinas—animal, plant, and ancestral spirits—play a major role in these ceremonies and are summoned to the village through dances. They are believed to inhabit the masked dancers who impersonate them, and the masks are treated as sacred objects.

Curriculum Context

Kachinas (spirits) are central to the beliefs and practices of many Native Americans.

Carved kachina dolls are given to children. All boys are initiated into the secret cults of the men's kivas by taking part in kachina dances. After the final dance, the adults swear the children to secrecy about the cult.

Sometimes, the dances are disrupted by the buffoonery of "kachina clowns," who are allowed to break the rules of good behavior. Their joking behavior acts as a useful safety-valve for tension within the village. At the same time, it reinforces the importance of proper social behavior within the community.

Salish

The Salish are a large group of Native Americans who speak dialects belonging to the Salish language family. There are two main subgroups of Salish, the Interior Salish—the subject of this chapter—and the Coast Salish, covered separately.

The Interior Salish once occupied the central and southern high Plateau area bordered by the Rocky Mountains to the east and the Coastal and Cascade Mountain ranges to the west. The area included part of what is now British Columbia, northern Washington, Idaho, and western Montana. The land, which varies from arid sagebrush country to forest, is drained by the Fraser, Thompson, and Columbia rivers and tributaries.

Tribes and traditions

Interior Salish tribes include the Lillooet, Cowlitz, Okanagon, Coeur d'Alene, Sanpoil, Shuswap, Flathead, Columbia, Kalispel, Sinkaiet or southern Okanagon, Spokane, Wenatchee, and Thompson. Lifestyles and traditions varied from one tribe to another, but all of them relied on salmon fishing as a main source of food and led a seminomadic lifestyle.

The different tribes spent the summer months in semipermanent villages situated near the great rivers, where they trapped salmon and gathered berries and, in some cases, roots. An abundant supply of food meant that some of it could be dried or otherwise preserved and stored for winter use.

As summer turned to fall, the Salish would travel to the mountains to hunt big game such as deer and moose, which supplied food as well as skins for clothing. Winter and early spring were spent in villages of earth lodges. In some areas, ice-fishing and hunting for small animals such as rabbit supplied fresh food that supplemented the staple diet of dried fish and berries.

Curriculum Context

Salish languages and lifestyles have some features in common but also many local differences.

Earth lodge

A partly subterranean circular building, covered with earth and with a dome-shaped roof and a smoke hole.

When food became scarce, the people were sometimes forced to rely on plant foods such as lichen.

Journeys between summer and winter camps were often on foot rather than by canoe. Travel by canoe—made from hollowed-out tree trunks—was often hazardous because of the many rapids in the rivers.

Contact with other tribes

Those tribes living on the eastern and western edges of their territory traded with, and to some degree were influenced by, neighboring tribes. For example, the Lillooet to the west traded with Northwest Coast peoples, including the Coast Salish, while the Flathead to the east traded with Plains tribes. It was the Plains tribes who introduced the Flathead to horse travel, and they became skilled horsemen. The Flathead also hunted buffalo and were warriors. The Salish of central regions, such as the Sanpoil, tended to be peaceful.

Curriculum Context

A study of Native American trade should examine interactions between neighboring tribes as well as with Europeans.

Contact with Europeans

The first contact between the Interior Salish and Europeans occurred in the early 19th century, when trappers and fur traders came from the east. They were followed in the 1850s by waves of settlers and prospectors searching for gold.

As the European population increased, wars broke out between Europeans and the Interior Salish. War, disease, European dominance, and the loss of traditional hunting and fishing grounds had a drastic effect on the Interior Salish. They not only reduced the native population but also brought about a decline in native culture and traditions. Since the beginning of the 20th century, most of the remaining Salish live on reservations in Canada and the United States. Many modern Salish earn a living as farmers, ranch hands, and ranch owners, as well as seasonal fishermen.

Tlingit

The Tlingit live on the coast and islands of southern Alaska. Together with the Haida, Tsimshian, and Haisla, they make up the northern group of the Northwest Coast people. All share a complex, hierarchical fishing-and-gathering culture based on wealth and status.

Before they first made contact with Europeans in the 18th century, the Tlingit numbered around 10,000 people. Because of the dense populations on the coast, fighting with neighboring tribes over land, particularly islands, was a constant feature of Tlingit life.

By the 1780s, the Tlingit were trading with the Russians, swapping furs for guns and iron. They fought frequently with the Russians who settled in Alaska in the early 19th century. During this period, European diseases and conflicts brought on by competition for trading goods severely reduced Tlingit numbers.

In 1971, the Tlingit and other tribes finally received some recompense, in the form of money and land from the Alaska Native Claims Settlement Act. Today, there are more than 14,000 Tlingit, many of whom work in the Alaskan logging and fishing industries.

Alaska Native Claims Settlement Act

A 1971 law in which Alaskan Native Americans gave up all their claims to land in return for 44 million acres (100,000 sq.km.) of land and $963 million, which were divided among 12 Native regional corporations and more than 200 village corporations.

A structured society

The basic Tlingit social unit is the lineage, with descent traced through the mother. Each lineage has its own chief, land, and ceremonies. Two or more lineages whose members can trace their descent from a common mythical ancestor make up a clan. Each clan has valued privileges, such as dances and masks, for ceremonies. Clan members belong to one of two moieties, Raven and Wolf—groups that cut across tribal boundaries. Marriage is always to someone outside one's own moiety.

This face is a detail from a Tlingit tribal house built in Haines, Alaska, in the 1950s. The house stands close to an arts center, where Tlingit arts and crafts are still practiced.

Slaves and salmon

Tlingit life was based around the activities of the most important families, who formed a class of nobles. Beneath them were the common people and then slaves, who were captured or traded from other tribes.

The Tlingit economy was based mainly on fishing for salmon with harpoons, nets, and traps. Fishing, hunting, and carving were men's work, while women picked berries and looked after the home.

The Tlingit used wood, especially cedar, to make everything from canoes to bowls. The women blended cedar bark with wool from mountain goats to weave their renowned Chilkat blankets.

Potlatches—ceremonies at which gifts were given to reaffirm social status—were central to Tlingit life. The greater the gathering, the greater the giver's status. They played a vital role at times of transition, such as the funeral of a clan chief. The new chief's family also gave a huge feast and gifts. By accepting his food and gifts, guests publicly recognized the new chief's status.

Like all Northwest Coast peoples, the Tlingit respected the animals they ate. Many of their religious practices were performed to placate animals' spirits so that other animals would let themselves be caught. Each year, the Tlingit thanked the first salmon they caught, then ritually returned the bones to the sea.

Curriculum Context

The Tlingit and other Northwest Coast Native American political systems can be compared with those in other regions of North America.

Toltec

The Toltec were a mixture of peoples who migrated north after the decline of the great city of Teotihuacan in southern Mexico about 950 CE. They settled in north, northwest, and central Mexico, establishing their capital at Tollan (Tula), about 250 miles (400 km) north of present-day Mexico City.

Curriculum Context

Students should be able to describe the major characteristics of Toltec peoples from their art and architecture.

Tula was built around a highland lake bed (the name means "place of reeds"). The ruins of its ceremonial center and the outlying housing districts indicate that Tula was a prosperous place. Ancient texts refer to buildings full of offerings (turquoise, shells, and feathers) brought from peoples over whom the Toltec ruled. Little is known about the early period of Tula's history apart from the existence of a cult of the god Quetzalcoatl and the presence of many skilled artisans.

The legend of Quetzalcoatl

References to Quetzalcoatl can be confusing, since it was both the name of a god and the name of one of the Toltec's first leaders. According to an ancient text called the *Annals of Cuauhtitlan*, a warrior called Mixcoatl had a son named Ce Acatl Topiltzin, who was also known as Quetzalcoatl. He was named after the Toltec god because he was wise and peaceable.

Quetzalcoatl helped found Tula, but followers of the warrior god Tezcatlipoca soon rose up and drove him out of the city. According to one legend, Quetzalcoatl reached the shores of the Gulf of Mexico, where he set himself on fire and became the Morning Star. He vowed to return one day to reclaim his kingdom.

Toltec and Maya

There is evidence from Mayan texts that a band of Toltec warriors seized the Mayan city of Chitchén Itzá soon after the foundation of Tula, forming a Toltec–Maya state. One of the buildings in Chitchén Itzá, the Temple of the Warriors, closely resembles the main temple at present-day Tula. The Castillo (or

Quetzalcoatl) pyramid and ball court (the largest in Mesoamerica) are also Toltec-influenced. Within two centuries, Chitchén Itzá was in ruins and many Toltec moved to highland Guatemala. According to the Popul Vuh, a Mayan text discovered in the 18th century, these Toltec were the ancestors of the Quiche Maya.

The height of the Toltec empire was during the 11th and 12th centuries, when the Toltec ruled much of central Mexico. But about 1170, Tula was attacked by fierce nomads (probably Chichimec) and the great city was reduced to ruins.

Later, the Aztecs viewed the Toltec empire as a golden age of peace and prosperity. When the Aztec leader Itzcoatl destroyed the old Aztec histories in 1428, he rewrote the Aztec genealogy (line of descent) to show them as the true heirs of the Toltec. Being a Toltec became identified with being civilized.

Popul Vuh

A book written around 1550 in the Quiche language, containing the history and myths of the Quiche in Guatemala.

Toltec

Language:	Nahuatl
Area:	Central Mexico
Population:	Approximately 60,000 in Tula about 1000 CE
Housing:	Stone houses
European contact:	None
Neighbors:	Chichimec, Mixtec, and Tononca
Lifestyle:	Farmers and warriors
Food:	Corn, beans, and squash
Crafts:	Sculptures, featherwork, and jewelry (gold and precious stones)

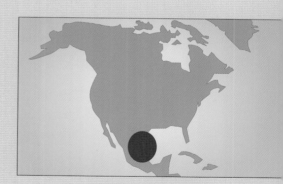

The influence of the Toltec empire spread across Mesoamerica.

The most important ruin at Tula (known as Temple B by archaeologists) includes several colossal columns over 15 feet (4.5 m) high that once supported a roof. They are made from four sections of basalt (volcanic rock) pegged together and feature carvings of warrior figures.

Ball court

A court on which the Mayan ball game took place. This game, which dates to at least 2,500 BCE, is believed to have had important ritual aspects and to have been used to settle disputes. Ball courts have been found from Arizona to Nicaragua, with more than 500 in Guatemala.

Art and architecture

There are very few written records to tell us about the Toltec. Most of what we know about these people comes from their art and architecture, which are dominated by images of warfare.

The ruins of Tula include the Burned Palace, two ball courts, and three stepped pyramid temples. Images around the temple include processions of jaguars and coyotes, eagles tearing at human hearts, and effigies (likenesses) of Quetzalcoatl. Around the temple and elsewhere in the ruins are the chacmools—reclining figures with bowls on their chests. These bowls may have received sacrificial offerings, although scholars do not believe the Toltec practiced human sacrifice on the same scale as the Aztecs.

Tsimshian

The Tsimshian live in 14 separate villages beside the Skeena and Nass rivers on the Pacific Coast of Alaska and British Columbia and on nearby islands. Each village name includes the word *Git* or *Kit* (meaning "people of "), followed by a name referring to the part of the river where the village stands.

The Tsimshian are closely related to other Northwest Coast groups, such as the Gitksan, whose legends say they come from a town in the interior of the United States called Temlaxam, or Prairie Town. The Tsimshian language may, however, be distantly related to Penutian, which is spoken by tribes living farther south, in the modern-day states of Washington, Oregon, and California.

Under one roof
Tsimshian homes are large, one-story houses made from wooden planks. Each has one main room with sleeping platforms built around the walls and a fireplace in the center. Partitioned off from this main living area is a smaller room at the back of the house. Here ceremonial items such as masks are kept when they are not being used.

As many as 30 or 40 people live in each house. The people in each house are all members of the same household clan—people who claim descent from a common legendary ancestor—together with other family members who have married into the clan. Tsimshian clans are matrilineal, meaning that people's kinships are determined through descent from their mothers.

Tsimshian life
The Tsimshian maintain a traditional way of life. Many of them work seasonally in the logging and fishing

> ### Curriculum Context
>
> North American peoples each have their own stories about their origins.

industries, but they still consider winter to be a sacred ceremonial season. There is also a strong revival of traditional crafts at villages such as Ksan, which has become a Tsimshian heritage craft and cultural center.

Although the Tsimshian live mostly on products from the sea and rivers, they also hunt in the inland forests for deer, bear, and mountain goats, and forage for wild foods, such as berries and roots. Fish is the Tsimshian's most important food, and the region has a plentiful supply. In spring, they fish for salmon and eulachon (candlefish), which swim up the rivers from the sea in great numbers. During the rest of the year, they catch fish such as halibut, cod, and flounder from the sea.

In the past, the Tsimshian also hunted sea mammals such as seals and sea otters, which provided materials for tools, clothes, and blankets, as well as food.

Tsimshian

Language:	Tsimshian
Area:	Coastal rivers and islands in British Columbia and Alaska
Reservation:	Village and island reservations in their traditional homeland
Population:	About 2,400 today
Housing:	One-story wooden houses
European contact:	Explorers, missionaries, and traders in the 18th and 19th centuries
Neighbors:	Tlingit and Haida
Lifestyle:	Based on fishing; live in settled villages
Food:	Fish, especially salmon; some game and wild foods such as berries
Crafts:	Memorial totem poles, copper ornaments and tools, woodwork, and basketry

The Tsimshian live beside two main rivers on the Northwest Coast.

The Tsimshian used to fish from dugout canoes, which they also used for transport, trading with neighboring tribes along the coast. One of their most important trade goods was eulachon oil, which came only from the Tsimshian area but was highly prized by other peoples on the coast. They obtained blankets woven from dog and goat hair from the Chilkat (a Tlingit people), which were richly decorated with animals and figures relating to clan totems. The skill of Tsimshian woodcarvers was such that there was wide trade demand for their masks and other items.

Curriculum Context

The trade interactions between peoples of the Northwest Coast are a revealing example of economic organization in Native American societies.

A class-based society

Tsimshian society, like that of other Northwest Coast tribes, is divided into classes. The highest class comprises heads of households, or chiefs. Below them are nobles, and beneath the nobles are common people. Before they were influenced by European ideals, the Tsimshian valued personal wealth highly, and many rich families adopted captives from other tribes. These captives were thought of as the property of their owners. They are sometimes referred to as slaves because they had few rights or privileges, but their lives were generally no more harsh than those of common Tsimshian people.

The spiritual life of the Tsimshian is complex. Like the Haida and Tlingit, they have powerful shamans (medicine men and women), who preside over the activities of secret societies. The most important of these are the Mitla (Those Who Descend from the Heavens) and Nutlem (Wolf Society).

Curriculum Context

Shamans are an essential part of Native American religious and spiritual life.

In the past when people were seriously ill, Tsimshian shamans tried to cure them by using hollow ivory tubes called "soul-catchers" in special rituals. This was because the Tsimshian traditionally believed that illness was caused by the soul, or spirit, leaving the body. They still use soul-catchers when someone is ill—performing such traditional rituals helps maintain tribal identity—but always in conjunction with modern medicine.

Tsimshian potlatches

Another tradition the Tsimshian retain is the holding of potlatches. These are celebrations at which a family holds a feast and claims ownership of masks, crests, and other privileges by giving out goods to its guests. By accepting the gifts, the guests recognize the claims of their hosts.

European contact

From the mid-1700s, the main European powers, especially Russia and England, sent expeditions along the Northwest Coast but did not try to settle there. They did trade with the Tsimshian, however, and by the 1780s, the exchange of sea-otter furs for metal goods had made the northern Northwest Coast a center of commerce. By the 1830s, the Hudson's Bay Company had trading posts in the area—although the fur trade had declined by then.

In the 1860s, William Duncan, a Scottish preacher, arrived with the aim of converting the Tsimshian to Christianity. Duncan studied their language and mythology and, in 1862, succeeded in converting several chiefs. He built a mission at Metlakatla, intending that the Tsimshian should give up their own culture and live in model villages of European-style houses, where they could learn skills such as carpentry and blacksmithing. He also set up a fish-canning factory and a sawmill.

In 1887, the British government decided to place the Tsimshian living in British Columbia on reservations. The Tsimshian appealed to Queen Victoria in vain and hired lawyers to protect their land rights. The court cases went on until 1927, when the Tsimshian were forbidden to pursue the matter any further.

Zuni

Speaking a distinct language unrelated to any other in the Southwest but possibly with distant links to Tanoan, the Zuni tribe live in a pueblo in northwestern New Mexico that they have inhabited for at least 600 years. Like the Hopi, Acoma, and Rio Grande Pueblo, the Zuni are farmers.

The Zuni's origins are shrouded in mystery, but it is thought they are descendants of the prehistoric Anasazi, merged with descendants of the Mogollon. They themselves believe they emerged from a sacred place underground. Members of religious cults still hold secret meetings in underground kivas.

Seven down to one

When first encountered by the Spanish in the 1500s, the Zuni were living in Hawikuh and a number of other villages—perhaps seven in all. These villages made up the fabled empire of gold, called the Seven Cities of Cibola, sought in vain by the Spanish conquistador, or conqueror, Francisco de Coronado.

The Pueblo Rebellion against the Spanish in 1680 resulted in Spanish atrocities against the Zuni and the tribe's consolidation in the 1690s into one settlement on the site of one of the original villages. But the Zuni's rich cultural and agricultural traditions survive among their 8,000–10,000 members today.

Seven Cities of Cibola

Legendary settlements whose riches inspired much early Spanish exploration of the Southwest.

Zuni crafts

Traditionally, Zuni men grew a wide variety of corn, peppers, squash, and cotton. They also wove cloth, while women made baskets and pots. Today, both men and women produce exquisite jewelry, particularly in silver and turquoise. Such crafts express the traditional Zuni view of the world, which is that people must live in harmony with nature.

Curriculum Context

Gender roles among the Zuni can be compared to those among other Native Americans.

Secret male societies

In common with many other tribes in the Southwest, Zuni society is organized into matrilineal clans, with descent passed on through female lines. However, the senior officers in the 13 Zuni clans are all male—as are all the members of the secret religious cults.

Membership in these cults is restricted, and new members have to undergo special initiation ceremonies. The cults organize the complex ceremonial life of the Zuni pueblo. It is based on ancestor worship and impersonations of a variety of gods and supernatural spirits called kachinas—particularly those that bring life-giving rain, such as Sayatasha, Rain Power of the North.

The Shalako Festival

The cults have their own priesthoods and are devoted to the worship of a particular group of gods and other

Zuni

Language:	Zuni
Area:	New Mexico
Reservation:	Northwestern New Mexico, south of Gallup
Population:	8,000–10,000 today
Housing:	Southwestern adobe (clay brick) houses
European contact:	Fray Marcos de Niza (Franciscan priest) in 1539
Neighbors:	Hopi, Navajo, and Acoma
Lifestyle:	Settled farmers
Food:	Corn, peppers, and cornmeal
Crafts:	Carving, jewelry, and pottery

The Zuni people live in northwestern New Mexico.

This photo of a Zuni woman and her elaborate jewelry was taken at the beginning of the 20th century. The Zuni are still famed for their jewelry.

supernatural spirits. For example, during the famous Shalako Festival (also called the House Blessing Ceremony), held in early winter, dancers (the Shalakos) move from house to house as they perform. They wear giant masks to represent the messengers of the rain gods coming down from the spirit world to bless new homes. The festival takes 10 months to prepare and lasts for 49 days. It is a reenactment of the Zuni's original emergence from underground and migration to their homeland. The Shalako Festival is also a time when the spirits of dead Zuni ancestors are believed to return to the world to be honored and fed by their living descendants.

Curriculum Context

Students learning about Native American religious beliefs and practices should include the study of secret cults and ancestor worship.

Glossary

Applegate Trail A wilderness trail from the eastern states to the Willamette Valley in Oregon, established in 1846 as a less dangerous route than the Oregon Trail. It branches from the Oregon Trail at Fort Hall, Idaho, and passes through the Nevada desert into northern California.

Ball court A court on which the Mayan ball game took place. This game, which dates to at least 2,500 BCE, is believed to have had important ritual aspects and to have been used to settle disputes.

Band A simple form of human society consisting of an extended kin or family group. Bands are smaller than tribes and have fewer social institutions.

Clan A social unit consisting of a number of households or families with a common ancestor.

Conquistador The Spanish word for "conqueror," used to describe the early Spanish soldiers, explorers, and adventurers involved in the conquest of the Americas.

Counting coup Among Plains peoples, an act of bravery in battle involving striking a blow against an enemy warrior's body with a decorated stick. The acts were recorded by making notches in the coup stick or by adding a feather to the warrior's headdress.

Dugout canoe A canoe hollowed out of a tree trunk.

Earth lodge A partly subterranean circular building, covered with earth and with a dome-shaped roof and a smoke hole.

Hogan A Navajo home, usually round and cone shaped, with a door facing east to welcome the rising Sun.

Hudson's Bay Company A trading company set up in 1670 in the Hudson Bay area of North America. It controlled the fur trade in the region for centuries, forming a network of trading posts and obtaining fur from local peoples in exchange for goods shipped from Britain.

Hunter–gatherers People who obtain most of their food by hunting wild animals and eating plants gathered from the wild.

Igloo A shelter made of blocks of snow, usually in the form of a dome. Igloos are built by Inuit in the Canadian central Arctic and in Greenland. The smallest are temporary shelters used on hunting trips. Larger ones are semipermanent, one-roomed family homes.

Kachina Spirit beings in the religion of Pueblo cultures. Dolls representing kachinas are carved and given to children to educate them. In ceremonial dances, people dress as kachinas.

Kayak A small boat used by Native Americans in Arctic regions to hunt on lakes, rivers, and in coastal waters. It was traditionally made from a driftwood frame covered with stitched animal skins.

Kiva An underground structure used for communal gathering, ceremonies, and councils, that is typical of early Anasazi settlements.

Longhouse A communal house shared by several families. Longhouses measured up to 200 feet (60 m) in length and were built of post frames covered in planks.

Long Walk The 300-mile (500 km) enforced trek of around 9,000 Navajo people from their homeland to Bosque Redondo in the Pecos River Valley. Around 200 people died on the 18-day journey.

Mission stations Religious outposts established by Spanish Roman Catholic priests to convert the indigenous people to Christianity.

Moiety One of two groups into which many Native American tribes were divided. Each was often composed of related clans, and marriage to someone of the same moiety was usually forbidden.

National Historic Landmark A structure, site, or district recognized by the U.S. government for its historical significance.

Oregon Trail A main migration route from the Mississippi River to Oregon, used between 1841 and 1869 before railroads were built.

Peyote The hallucinogenic peyote cactus of Texas and Mexico has been used in religious ceremonies and for healing by Native Americans for more than 2,000 years. Members of the Native American Church use it today in their religious practices.

Plank housing Housing of the Northwest Coast peoples, made from the cedar tree. Vertical cedar logs are clad with planks harvested from still-living trees. The planks are tied to the logs with cedar ropes and can be taken down and carried on seasonal migrations. The roof is also made of cedar wood.

Platform mound An earthwork created to support a structure or an activity.

Potlatch A ceremony common to several Native American societies of the Northwest Coast, in which an important person hosts a feast for guests. Relationships within and between clans and villages are reinforced, and the host demonstrates his wealth and raises his status by giving away gifts.

Pyramid A building with triangular outer surfaces that converge to a point. Mesoamericam pyramids are usually stepped with temples at the top.

Reservation An area of land set aside for a specific Native American group, governed by a tribal council and with its own laws. Its contact with the federal government is through the Bureau of Indian Affairs.

Shaman A person with special powers to access the spirit world and an ability to use magic to heal the sick and control events.

Sun Dance An important ceremony practiced by Plains peoples to celebrate the renewal of nature.

Tepee A cone-shaped tent built with a pole framework and traditionally covered with animal skins.

Totem pole Sculptures carved from large trees by tribes of the Northwest Coast. The designs illustrate legends or important events, clan lineages, or shamanic powers.

Umiak A large boat, similar in construction to a kayak, made for use in Arctic coastal areas by indigenous peoples. It can hold around 20 people and is used to transport people and their possessions and for hunting whales and walrus.

Wickiup The Southwestern or Western name for a domed dwelling consisting of a single room, formed on a frame of arched poles and covered with a roofing material such as birchbark, grass, or hides (*see* Wigwam).

Wigwam The Eastern name for a domed dwelling consisting of a single room, formed on a frame of arched poles and covered with a roofing material such as birchbark, grass, or hides (*see* Wickiup).

Further Research

BOOKS

Cheewa, James. *Modoc: The Tribe That Wouldn't Die.* Naturegraph Publishers, 2008.

Coe, Michael D., and Rex Koontz. *Mexico: From the Olmecs to the Aztecs.* Thames & Hudson, 2008.

Frank, L., and Kim Hogeland. *First Families: Photographic History of California Indians.* Heyday Books, 2007.

Iverson, Peter. *Dine: A History of the Navajos.* University of New Mexico Press, 2002.

Johansen, Bruce E. *The Native Peoples of North America: A History.* Rutgers University Press, 2006.

Johnson, Michael. *Encyclopedia of Native Tribes of North America.* Firefly Books, 2007.

Keegan, Marcia. *Pueblo People: Ancient Traditions, Modern Lives.* Clear Light Publishing, 1999.

Nerburn, Kent. *Chief Joseph & the Flight of the Nez Perce: The Untold Story of an American Tragedy.* HarperOne, 2006.

Page, Suzanne, and Jake Page. *Hopi.* Rio Nuevo Publishers, 2009.

Philip, Neil. *The Great Circle: A History of the First Nations.* Clarion Books, 2006.

Pritzker, Barry M., ed. *A Native American Encyclopedia: History, Culture & Peoples.* Oxford University Press, USA, 2000.

Sandos, James A. *Converting California: Indians and Franciscans in the Missions.* Yale University Press, 2008.

Sharer, Robert, and Loa Traxler. *The Ancient Maya.* Stanford University Press, 2005.

Smith, Michael E. *The Aztecs.* Wiley-Blackwell, 2002.

Stuart, David E. *Anasazi America: Seventeen Centuries on the Road from Center Place.* University of New Mexico Press, 2000.

Thornton, Thomas F. *Being and Place Among the Tlingit.* University of Washington Press, 2007.

Waldman, Carl, and Molly Braun. *Encyclopedia of Native American Tribes.* Facts on File, 2006.

INTERNET RESOURCES

The Canadian Encyclopedia. Articles on each of Canada's First Peoples and on peoples of the Arctic, Subarctic, Eastern Woodland, Plateau, Plains, and Northwest Coast.
www.thecanadianencyclopedia.com

Carnegie Museum of Natural History. North, South, East, West: American Indians and the Natural World examines Tlingit, Iroquois, Hopi, and Lakota interactions with the natural world.
www.carnegiemnh.org/exhibits/north-south-east-west/

DesertUSA. This Guide to the American Southwest and Desert Regions has a section on peoples and cultures with many articles on Native American Indians, ancient peoples, rock art, and Spanish explorers and missionaries.
www.desertusa.com

EMuseum@Minnesota State University. Its Prehistory section includes detailed sections on the Aztecs, Mayans, Olmecs, and Toltecs.
www.mnsu.edu/emuseum/prehistory/latinamerica/meso/cultures

Indian Pueblo Cultural Center. Information on the 19 Pueblo peoples of New Mexico, their history, and arts and crafts.
www.indianpueblo.org

National Museum of the American Indian. The Smithsonian Institution's National Museum of the American Indian website. The site provides information about the museum's collections as well as educational resources.
www.nmai.si.edu/

Native American History. Site from the University of Washington with links to information on all aspects of Native American history.
www.lib.washington.edu/subject/history/tm/native.html

NativeAmericans.com. A comprehensive site with information and links about all aspects of Native American culture and history, including online biographies, extensive bibliographies, and information about the history and culture of Native American groups.
www.nativeamericans.com

Native Americans Documents Project. Provides access to documents relating to Native American history, including federal Indian policy and the Dawes General Allotment Act.
www2.csusm.edu/nadp/

NorthWestCoast Indians. Photos and descriptions of Northwest Coast historical artifacts.
www.northwestcoastindian.com

Smithsonian: American Indian History and Culture. A Smithsonian Institution website, with information about all aspects of Native American history and culture.
www.si.edu/Encyclopedia_SI/History_and_Culture/AmericanIndian_History.htm

Index

Page numbers in *italic* refer to illustrations.